SWITCH OFF OVERTHINKING

33 WAYS TO CALM YOUR THOUGHTS, REDUCE STRESS, STOP NEGATIVE SPIRALS, AND IMPROVE MENTAL CLARITY

CHASE HILL

CONTENTS

A FREE GIFT TO OUR READERS

29 WAYS TO OVERCOME NEGATIVE THOUGHTS

I'd like to give you a gift as a way of saying thanks for your purchase!

In 29 Ways to Overcome Negative Thoughts, you'll discover:

- 10 Strategies to Reduce Negativity in Your Life
- 7 Steps to Quickly Stop Negative Thoughts

- 12 Powerful Tips to Beat Negative Thinking

To receive your Free Ebook, visit the link:

free.chasehillbooks.com

Alternatively, you can scan the QR-code below:

If you have any difficulty downloading the ebook, contact me at **chase@chasehillbooks.com**, and I'll send you a copy as soon as possible.

INTRODUCTION

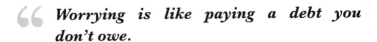 *Worrying is like paying a debt you don't owe.*

MARK TWAIN

Anna woke up on Monday morning trembling with fear and dripping with sweat. Looking over at the clock, she noticed it was only 5 a.m., but she knew she could kiss goodbye for the next couple of hours before the alarm went off.

Instead, she would lie in bed, urging herself to switch off and accept the need for sleep. However, her mind had other intentions! It would remind her of the presentation she was due to give at work that week. More specifically, her brain would torment her with images of tripping in front of her colleagues, losing her notes, or being asked questions to which she didn't have the answers.

By the time Anna had to get up, she was already mentally and physically exhausted. After all, this wasn't the first morning her brain had tortured her like this. Each day was filled with increasing levels of fatigue and anxiety, which only led to more problems at work, fueling this cycle of thoughts where failure was the only outcome.

Anna was aware that she was getting tense and worked up over a problem that didn't even exist, a skill she had mastered! But no matter how many times she reminded herself of this, she couldn't break free from overthinking.

It didn't just stop with work. She would replay conversations she had had with friends. After writing a message, she would delete it multiple times because the wording never seemed quite right. And when that person didn't reply, she would worry even more. She would overthink what to cook, what to do in her free time, and even what to watch on TV. It was exhausting to the point where it became easier to withdraw from life as much as possible.

Aside from the unbearable amount of stress, overthinking can be unimaginably isolating. Loved ones attempt to help by offering words of wisdom such as "You are overthinking" and "It's never as bad as you think it is." You smile and agree, but on the inside, you just want to thank them for stating the blindingly obvious. In the end, it's easier just to keep these problems to yourself.

Despite greater awareness of mental health, society still seems to frown on expressing emotions. If we could break free from the need to suppress our thoughts and feelings, it would become clear how many people suffer from overthinking.

Research has shown that 73 percent of 25 to 35-year-olds suffer from chronic overthinking, and 52 percent of people between the ages of 45 and 55 are going through the same (Santilli, 2023). To put this in perspective, if you are in a room with ten other people, the chances are high that six of them are going through similar struggles as you.

Overthinking and being trapped in these savage loops of negativity lead to more than stress and anxiety. These patterns can make even the simplest of decisions hard to make. The thought of making a life-changing decision is enough to cause decision paralysis, missed opportunities, and a series of regrets. Without the energy to handle life's stressors, you are left feeling burned out.

But again, we are living in a world where stress is considered normal. Overthinking and the series of events that follow rob us of the joy of life, of living in the moment and thriving in our everyday interactions. Not only do you struggle to sit and enjoy a coffee or a trip to the park with your children, but you also feel guilty for those rare moments of happiness!

The irony is that trying to overcome overthinking will likely cause more overthinking as you doubt whether you have the physical and emotional strength to take on such a challenge. Nevertheless, you know that it is something that must be conquered.

By taking control of your overthinking, you can calm the turbulence caused by your racing mind, allowing you to effectively and confidently make decisions while becoming more productive in your personal and professional life.

You will feel the benefits of emotional resilience so that you have what it takes to handle the inevitable stress that comes your way. And once you discover the techniques to manage anxiety and negative thoughts, you can start reveling in a life full of bliss!

It still seems all too far out of reach, doesn't it? This is where the unique SWITCH OFF method comes into play. Each with its own chapter, this method allows you to:

- **S**: Seek Clarity

- **W**: Wellness Integration

- **I**: Inner Strength

- **T**: Transformative Creativity

- **C**: Conscious Nourishment

- **H**: Healthy Limits

- **O**: Optimal Choices

- **F**: Firm Habits

- **F**: Future Focus

This 9-step process guides you through actionable steps combined with a holistic approach that you can simply integrate into daily life. We will begin by understanding more about overthinking triggers and patterns before covering a wealth of mind-body practices as we work toward an empowered future where aspirations are reached.

I have been fortunate to see the SWITCH OFF method bring about some amazing life changes for myself and while working as a life coach. It was my own challenges with overthinking that first led me to this career.

Switch Off Overthinking takes a different approach to my previous book *How to Stop Overthinking*. You can begin with the first strategy in chapter one or with a technique you feel will bring about the most benefits.

After all, while we have overthinking in common, we are still all very much individuals, and it's important to use the SWITCH OFF method to create your personalized journey. That being said, I do encourage you to work through all of the strategies in your own time!

What I love so much about the SWITCH OFF method is that you don't need anything to get started.

The two most essential things that will steer you through the path to mental freedom are your commitment to a short amount of time each day and your engagement in the activities in each chapter. Aside from this, the only thing I encourage you to have is a journal for self-reflection nearby.

There is no need to feel overwhelmed. You are dealing with real and complex thought patterns, and this is why there is no need to rush through the chapters. You will start to feel the difference even as we dive straight into the first chapter.

So be patient with yourself, be compassionate with yourself, and let's get started!

CHAPTER ONE: S: SEEK CLARITY

Our minds are the most incredible mass of intelligence and function. You only have to stop and consider all the unconscious actions our body carries out on a 24/7 basis to marvel at its mechanics.

In addition to that, our conscious thoughts, such as the decisions we make in our daily lives and the ability to recall information to carry out our jobs, are also added.

To add to the brain's workload, there are also thoughts that serve no real use—those negative thoughts that hound us, interrupting the thoughts that actually have a purpose.

There has been a lot of interest in the number of thoughts a person has in a single day, and it is easy to feel confused when you read 6,000 in one source and 60,000 in another. To understand this difference better, it's crucial to clarify what different experts classify as a thought.

A 2020 study calculated that the average person has 6,000 thoughts per day, but this is subjective. The number was based on a median of 6.5 thought transitions or "thought worms" per minute. This takes into consideration the average of 8 hours of sleep per night, and fewer hours would amount to more thought worms.

The concept of thought worms is also interesting. A thought worm is considered to be a new thought. Those who have estimated upwards of 60,000 thoughts per day base their results on the idea that there are numerous "mini thoughts" before a new thought is generated within each thought worm.

These numbers are overwhelming enough, but of those thousands of thoughts, differing research suggests that anywhere from 75 to 90 percent are negative thoughts. No wonder you and many others find it hard to see past the weight of overthinking.

Thinking is a tricky process, both conscious and subconscious. It's something we think (ironically) we have control over, but in fact, there is so much going on in our minds that the ability to control our thoughts is drowned out by the constant chatter.

Before attempting to regain mental control, it's necessary to delve into why your brain seems to insist on torturing you!

STRATEGY #1: UNDERSTANDING THE FOUNDATIONS OF OVERTHINKING

Everyone has moments when their thoughts seem to completely take over, especially in times of stress, but overthinking takes this to an excessive point. It's almost impossible to focus or think about anything else. Overthinking is rarely helpful.

On the contrary, it negatively impacts mental health, even leading to anxiety and depression. For some, overthinking can spiral out of control and develop into sleep disorders, generalized anxiety disorder, obsessive-compulsive disorder, social anxiety disorder, panic disorder, or post-traumatic stress disorder.

If you stop to consider the one thing that last got caught in your mind, you will probably notice that it is something that happened in the past or something that may happen in the future, neither of which are helpful in the present. This leaves you in a constant state of worry, unable to relax.

The negative thoughts that get played over and over in your mind lead to mental exhaustion. It's a nasty cycle because the more you ruminate on these experiences, real or not, the worse your mental health becomes and the harder it becomes to stop overthinking.

Decision-making can be significantly impaired. You may find that you come to a decision, but there is always something nagging at the back of your mind, causing you to doubt your decision and rethink everything. This is both exhausting and time-consuming. In some cases, the options are so overwhelming that analysis paralysis occurs, making action impossible.

When a decision is finally made, it can be extremely frustrating when you spend even more time beating yourself up for the choice you made. The decision may have been the right one, but that doesn't stop you from thinking that things could have been done better.

To get a clear understanding of your overthinking, answer the following statements with a simple yes or no. Nobody will think more or less of you based on your answers, so be as honest as possible.

1. When I say something, I spend a lot of time thinking about my answer.
2. When someone says, "I need to talk to you," I become anxious.
3. I say sorry when things aren't my fault.
4. It takes a long time to fall asleep when I go to bed because my brain won't stop.
5. If I do something embarrassing, I can't stop thinking about it.
6. I am convinced there are hidden meanings behind everything people say.
7. I often miss what people say to me because I get lost in my thoughts.
8. My mind is often consumed with future scenarios that I miss out on the present.
9. Daily tasks become difficult because my mind is preoccupied with other thoughts.
10. Many moments in the day are spent on "what-ifs."

The main problem with overthinking is that there is usually little to no evidence to support the repetitive thought. These types of thought patterns are called cognitive distortions. Review the list below and decide if any of the following sound familiar:

• **Black-and-white-thinking:** You are considering a situation as either all good or all bad.

- **Catastrophizing:** You think that things are far worse than they are like your presentation didn't go well, so you believe you are about to lose your job.

- **Overgeneralizing:** You expect the outcome of a situation to be the same as a past event, ruling out the possibility that there are a number of other ways for things to turn out.

- **Filtering:** All the positives are filtered out of the equation, and you only focus on the negatives.

- **Jumping to conclusions:** You might interpret a situation with negative thoughts and make assumptions without all the information, leading you to jump to the wrong conclusion.

- **Personalization:** You blame yourself for everything, even things that are beyond your control. You may also take other people's beliefs and opinions personally.

- **Should statements:** You tell yourself that you should be doing things differently, better, or in a certain way without allowing exceptions.

It's crucial for you to understand that overthinking is not an intentional action. As much as people try to tell you to just think about something else or be a little more positive, it's not the case. The first step to overcoming the cycle of rumination is to recognize that this is an automatic form of self-protection.

Thousands of years ago, our ancestors would have been walking through the forest in search of food. A rattle in the leaves ahead could have meant one of two things: predator or prey. The sound could have come from a rabbit or a saber-toothed tiger. Our ancestors' brains were wired to think negatively, and their survival depended on it. Unfortunately, this negativity bias has stuck with us, even though the same dangers aren't always present.

The power of the negativity bias shouldn't be overlooked or minimized. You have probably spent a long time judging yourself because of your overthinking, fueling the cycle. From this point on, I urge you to remind yourself that this is your brain's way of protecting you.

Nevertheless, you can retrain your brain to work in your favor!

Throughout the SWITCH OFF method, you will become more aware of what causes overthinking, and generally, there are three main causes.

Stress is a major factor. The levels of stress we are under today are far from normal or healthy, and stress management techniques will help. Many people struggle with self-doubt and a lack of self-esteem, leading to a stream of thoughts about decisions and actions. Perfectionism is another potential cause of overthinking.

Aside from self-compassion to compensate for judgment, you will also need a decent amount of patience. The problem of overthinking didn't develop overnight, meaning it will not go away in the same time frame. The focus of the first strategy is to get more comfortable recognizing your thoughts and labeling them for what they really are.

Throughout the day, take a few moments to notice when overthinking takes over. Use the following points to track these thoughts, become aware of your emotional response, and decide if they fall into a cognitive distortion category.

Situation (what happened?)	Thought	Behavior/Reaction	Alternative Thought
My partner is mad	I have done something wrong, they are going to leave me, and I'm going to be alone forever	Feelings of sadness, distraught, walking on eggshells, trying too hard to please when it's not necessary	My partner has had a tough day and needs some space

By doing this for a few days, you will be in a better position to understand not only your overthinking but whether or not there are any particular patterns.

STRATEGY #2: IDENTIFY TRIGGERS AND PATTERNS

Imagine you are walking down the street feeling okay about life when you notice a smell that fills you with overwhelming emotion. This is known as a trigger, an emotional response that doesn't fit the present situation. Triggers seem to come out of nowhere but have the habit of leaving you dismayed and shaken up.

Emotional triggers can be caused by past events, memories, fear, stress, relationship troubles, and change. Emotional triggers can prompt rumination. In the case of the smell in the street, it could have triggered a memory from a neglectful home during childhood or even a wonderful holiday, as they don't always have to be negative.

With regards to overthinking, triggers can lead to panic, increased heartbeat, difficulty breathing, the inability to control your emotions, the urge to escape the situation, and negative thoughts!

Identifying the triggers and patterns of your overthinking can significantly help you feel more prepared when the cycle starts, even stopping it before it gets out of hand.

Choice Overload

We are faced with hundreds of decisions daily, some trivial and others more significant. But even something as simple as deciding what to eat when there are so many options can tax the brain.

It's only in recent history that this paradox of choices has caused so much overthinking. In the past, we had fewer options. Our stores had fewer products, career choices weren't as vast, and marriage and children were almost assumed.

On the outside, more choices seem beneficial; however, the opposite is true, and more often than not, decision fatigue occurs. More variety makes decision-making harder, and expectations for the chosen option are higher.

There is a lot of stress over making the wrong decision and the potential for regret. Sometimes, you may not know exactly what you are looking for and overthink things that you aren't even certain about.

Uncertain Situations

Humans are creatures of habit and routine as they provide us with a sense of stability, and in many cases, routines reduce choice overload. When your day ahead is planned, there are fewer options to drain your cognitive abilities.

Nevertheless, there will be change and uncertainty, and all of a sudden, instead of embracing the change, you have already imagined the worst-case scenario.

Catastrophizing is one of the most common cognitive distortions, and we are all guilty of it at some point, but not to the extent that it disrupts our mental health.

Imagine if your boss calls an emergency meeting or your child's teacher emails for a meeting. Neither is part of your plan, and you must rearrange your schedule.

Even if you don't need to do anything for the uncertain situation, you still feel unprepared and anxious.

Procrastination and Perfectionism

Whether it's the influence of society or our own incredibly high expectations, many have reached a point where mistakes aren't just embarrassing but completely unacceptable. Striving for perfection leaves you feeling that nothing is good enough and, ultimately, mistakes were made. Even perceived mistakes and flaws can cause a lack of sleep, increased stress, and overthinking.

Procrastination is similar to choice overload but it's less about making decisions and more about a lack of taking action. You might tell yourself you have time to do a task later or that you work better under stress. You might need to reorganize your to-do list instead of getting on with doing it.

In relation to perfectionism, it's purposely and unnecessarily postponing doing something or making a decision for fear of not being perfect.

Fear of Conflict

If you're afraid of something, like conflicts or dogs, remember that fearing every confrontation or every dog leads to avoidance, not to mention treating all as if they are the same. This avoidance prevents you from practicing how to overcome your fear. If you don't have the opportunity to practice conflict management skills, you will end up facing more conflicts.

Avoiding conflicts is mentally exhausting, leaving you to walk on eggshells. Each potential interaction can lead you to overthink the conversation itself and the outcomes or consequences. Without the right skills, assuming all conflicts will end in disaster is normal.

Social Comparisons

Since the emergence of mass media, people have fallen into the trap of comparing themselves to others. Beauty magazines took much of the blame, and then the criticism shifted to social media. When scrolling through images and videos of individuals who seemingly have a perfect life, it's easy to forget that those posting are only choosing images they want others to see.

This type of social compassion is called upward social comparison, which can motivate you to improve your life, which isn't a bad thing until envy or jealousy arises.

This is one trigger of stress and overthinking, but downward social comparison can spur overthinking too.

Seeing a person who is worse off than yourself can cause you to feel better about your own situation. Though this gives you a chance to shed a new perspective on your life, there may also be feelings of guilt and the need to do more.

I have heard people say that they are lucky because they have a roof over their heads and food on the table despite suffering terrible losses in their own lives. On the outside, this is true, but it only leads to emotional suppression and further turmoil. You are entitled to feel any type of emotion regarding your situation.

Past Experiences

This trigger often goes back to our negativity bias. When thinking about the past, it's easier to remember the bad moments over the good, the mistakes over the successes, and even the insults over the compliments. The pain that these experiences cause can soar in line with rumination, each time becoming more distressing.

Ruminating about the past isn't the same as worrying about a problem or decision. It is also different from obsessing over an irrational thought or fear. The intense emotions that arise from reliving our past can increase the risk of mental health conditions or exacerbate existing conditions.

Strategy #1 was all about tracking thoughts as they arise. This strategy involves taking time to explore thoughts through journaling.

Journaling is an excellent therapeutic practice that allows you to express yourself without fear of judgment, become more self-aware, and declutter the mind.

Journaling doesn't come easily to everyone, so the following journal prompts can help you explore the triggers of overthinking.

1. What is your biggest fear or worry that causes you to overthink?
2. What is your worst-case scenario? How likely is it to happen on a scale of 1 to 10?
3. In five years, will the thing you are overthinking about be relevant?
4. If you had no fears, how would you handle the situation you are overthinking?
5. What three things are more important to you than your current overthinking situation?
6. List three things you overthink about but are completely out of your control.
7. How is overthinking affecting your relationships, personal and professional?
8. Create an alter ego. How would your alter ego handle your overthinking?
9. What is your current coping method for overthinking?
10. Describe a time when overthinking caused you to misread or judge a person or situation.

While journaling is a good place to begin your journey into greater self-awareness, mindfulness is far from the latest buzzword. For moments of overthinking, learning how to bring your focus to the present is an essential skill!

STRATEGY #3: MINDFUL AWARENESS

It is impossible for anyone to clear their mind of thoughts completely, and this is a huge misconception about mindfulness and meditation that can put off many individuals.

Mindfulness is about being fully aware of the present moment, which involves knowing where you are and what is happening around you. What makes mindfulness challenging for some is not to be reactive or overwhelmed by these moments.

Mindfulness and mindful meditation allow you to observe your thoughts and feelings without judging them. It can reduce mental chatter, lower stress levels, and improve sleep. What used to be considered a little hippy has now been proven to lessen symptoms of anxiety and depression.

For an overthinker, the idea of being able to sit with thoughts and not let them take over can seem like something unachievable, but it is a skill that can be learned and developed. There are many different ways to practice mindfulness and we will discuss more throughout the different strategies.

In the beginning, try not to set your expectations too high, and I say this from personal experience. You may have heard of people sitting for half an hour or even an hour in their meditative state, but meditation experts recommend no more than 15 to 20 minutes at a time.

It's the first few minutes when you will experience the biggest benefits, so it's best to start with no more than 3 to 5 minutes.

The 5, 4, 3, 2, 1, Technique

This is the perfect place to start because your brain is engaging all the senses in the present.

Take a moment to look around and find five things you can see. It could be anything from the color of the walls to the picture hanging on the wall.

Now, let's move on to touch. Find four things you can reach out and touch. It could be the texture of your clothes, the smooth surface of your desk, or the warmth of a cup of coffee.

Next up, listen closely for three things you can hear. It might be the hum of your computer, the distant sound of traffic outside, or the gentle rustle of leaves if you're outdoors.

Now, focus on smell. Find two scents in your surroundings. It could be the warm aroma of spices from the kitchen or the gentle scent of flowers in the room.

Finally, take a moment to notice one thing you can taste. It could be the rich bitterness of dark chocolate melting on your tongue or the tangy burst of citrus from a slice of lemon.

This sensory experience pulls your attention to your environment rather than to thoughts that take over. Make your brain work! Don't just say the first things that come to mind. Challenge your senses. Look for the cracks in a wall or the sounds beyond the bustle of traffic outside your window.

That's not to say that thoughts won't appear, and this is okay and normal! When thoughts appear, imagine them as an object, a leaf, a wave, or anything related to you. Picture the thought attached to your objective, recognize that it's there, but then allow it to move past you.

I found it useful to imagine a cloud in the wind, the thought coming closer, but the wind blowing it passed me. Once the cloud had passed, I went back to the grounding technique.

Getting Comfortable with Being Uncomfortable

This technique might feel counterintuitive, but it helps with avoidance. More often than not, overthinking can cause intense and overwhelming emotions. In an attempt to not feel these feelings, you might push your thoughts away. Keep in mind that your thoughts and feelings can't hurt you. Instead of avoiding them, learning how to sit with them is good practice.

Set a timer for a few minutes and allow yourself to feel all of that discomfort. Pay attention to how this discomfort feels in your body, such as tension or tingling. This time will help you better understand where your feelings come from.

Please bear in mind that if sitting with your discomfort causes extreme distress or you notice the symptoms of a panic attack, you should stop. It's not that the strategy doesn't work; it just means that more work needs to be done on your physical reaction to stress and anxiety, which we will cover later.

Guided Meditation

If you struggle to remain in the present, guided meditation lets you follow a voice that prompts you throughout your meditation, reminding you to focus on your breath or helping you visualize your goal.

There are thousands of guided meditations online, with a range of objectives from overthinking to building self-esteem. Some last 5 to 10 minutes, while others can last over an hour. Like all mindful activities, longer doesn't necessarily mean greater effects. Mental chatter starts to calm during mindful awareness, but the next strategy helps to quiet that buzzing for improved clarity.

STRATEGY #4: MENTAL DECLUTTERING

Do you ever reach a point when your brain feels so full that you have reached your capacity, and any additional information could push you over the edge? When your brain is overloaded, it makes it harder to recall information, leading to forgetfulness and mistakes.

Brain Dump

An amazing activity to declutter the mind is to do a brain dump. This requires just a pen and paper and a timer. Set the timer to 5 or 10 minutes, which is enough time for most people, and dump all of your thoughts onto the paper. There is no need to worry about handwriting, grammar, or spelling. There is no need to filter your thoughts. Imagine it's like the trash can on your computer—emptying it frees up space!

Organize Your Thoughts

Every day, we create lists of things that need to be done, either mentally or written down in to-do lists. The tasks are then prioritized.

Throughout this chapter, there have been opportunities to write down thoughts. It's now time to organize them. Organizing thoughts has many benefits similar to to-do lists.

It allows you to be more productive by prioritizing what is important. It keeps you more focused and in the present, enabling work-life balance. While calming the mind, you may also notice that you feel better about yourself too.

Revisit the thoughts that play on your mind and rank them from 1 to 5 as priorities. This will help you to discover which thoughts need urgent attention and which can be delayed.

Here are a few more ways you can help declutter the mind:

- **Stop multitasking:** You may think that doing more tasks at once equals more productivity, but it gives the brain multiple challenges at once, and things actually end up taking longer.

- **Schedule in time for worrying:** if you know your mind is going to revert to constant chatter, schedule short breaks during the day for this to happen. Overthinking won't be a problem forever, but as you work through the strategies, scheduled worry time can prevent worrying from becoming your entire day.

- **Offload your thoughts:** Whether it's a trusted friend or family member, or an online support group, talking to others about your concerns can lighten your load and provide you with a different perspective.

- **Physically declutter:** Keep your workspace and home environment clutter-free. Physical clutter in your surroundings takes up mental space and can lead to mental clutter in the form of information overload and a lack of focus.

• **Spend time in nature:** Many studies have proven that nature can help reduce stress, anxiety, and depression. Time in nature also gives you moments to engage your senses and enjoy the present moment.

• **Take breaks:** Not a break from work to fold laundry or a break from the children to catch up on emails. Take real breaks that allow your mind and body to disconnect from what you are doing. We have come to live in a world where we feel guilty if we aren't doing anything, and it shouldn't be like this!

Now that you are more aware of the types of overthinking and the triggers that can cause this exhausting habit, it's time to move on to our next set of strategies that will highlight how overthinking isn't just something that affects the mind but the whole body.

CHAPTER TWO: W: WELLNESS INTEGRATION

Overthinking leads to stress, which affects both the mind and body. At the same time, recognizing the mind-body connection can alleviate a wealth of problems.

Research showed how 20 minutes of exercise can improve a person's mood for up to 12 hours (The University of Vermont, 2018). Let's dive straight into the striking relationship between the mind and body.

STRATEGY #5: THE MIND-BODY CONNECTION

There is a romanticized idea that our feelings come from the heart, whereas our thoughts are generated in the mind. Due to the extensive connections between the brain, the endocrine, and the immune system, there is technically no separation of the body and mind.

This is evident in the way we physically feel our emotions, from butterflies in the stomach to shaking with anger. The body and mind shouldn't be seen as two separate entities but as one that functions together, with the body influencing the mind and emotions and vice versa.

Interestingly, scientists asked 701 people from different backgrounds to map where they felt increased or decreased activity in their bodies depending on different emotions. Despite the cultural differences of the participants, emotional activity was incredibly similar.

Fear and anxiety were more predominant in increased activity in the head and core of the body. There was a decrease in activity in the limbs when depression and sadness were experienced, but sadness also showed an increase in activity in the chest.

Surprise and shame had similar results, with increased activity in the head and chest but decreased activity in the legs. Only happiness showed an increase in activity over the entire body (Dean, 2023).

The science behind the mind and body connection will be revealed later on, but for now, let's look at relatable connections.

One day, you wake up, and the sun is shining; you slept well, and you begin your day with a quick workout, a refreshing shower, and the ultimate morning drink while you plan your day. As a result, problems are easier to handle, you have more energy, and interactions are more meaningful.

However, the next day, overthinking kept you awake for most of the night. You dread the day ahead. The extra energy you need to focus leaves you feeling drained by midday, so you reach for a sugary snack to give you a boost. That works for half an hour, but then you come crashing down again with no motivation for the rest of the day. You feel frustrated with yourself and spend the entire evening ruminating.

The mind-body connection is intuitive. If you put on your favorite warm sweater on a cold day, you feel happier, not just because of the additional heat but because of the sense of comfort. Whether we choose to pay attention to the connection is another matter. It becomes easier to notice how closely the two are entwined when strengthening this connection.

There are various forms of exercise and even devices that can increase your mind-body awareness; however, if you don't have enough time for these just yet, here is a simple way to start each day with greater awareness of this powerful connection:

Mind-Body 5-Minute Morning Routine

Step 1: When you wake up, spend a minute noticing how your body feels, not just the aches and pains but also areas that are relaxed and free from tension.

Step 2: Take a deep breath and visualize the oxygen entering your lungs, passing into the bloodstream, and feeding your organs, providing you with essential energy.

Step 3: Notice your emotions. What are you looking forward to or not looking forward to? Don't give the negatives any more attention than the positives or blow them out of proportion. Simply notice the emotions they cause.

Step 4: As soon as you get up, slowly drink a glass of water, knowing that you are starting your day by providing your body with what it needs.

Step 5: Set one intention for your day that will have a positive effect on both your mind and body, whether replacing a coffee with a green tea or going for a 5-minute walk during a break.

When you have more time, even if it's just 10 minutes, you can try integrating one or more of the following activities into your day.

Mindfulness and Meditation

When paying attention to the present, you can be more in tune with your emotions and even the physical response. By recognizing that you feel anxious, the brain sends the necessary messages for the body to calm down. To enhance the mind-body connection through guided meditation, you can try a YouTube video such as the one by Deepak Chopra.

Deepak Chopra: A Guided Meditation: The Mind-Body Connection

Yoga and Tai Chi

These exercises are steeped with tradition and can be done at home with the help of apps or online videos or by taking classes. Both exercises combine a focus on breathing with heart rate and muscle awareness, synchronizing breathwork with movement. They can help to calm the mind while strengthening the body, reducing stress, and improving self-esteem.

Dancing

This one may come as a surprise, but similarly to yoga, dancing allows you to switch off the external buzzing and connect with your inner rhythm. It's the perfect moment for self-expression while getting some physical activity.

There is no need to worry about following certain dance moves like you would in Zumba unless you want to. You can just play your favorite music and dance...with no one watching!

Biofeedback

Biofeedback techniques enable you to control some of your body's responses, such as heart rate, breathing, and muscle tension, through the use of electrical pads that give your feedback.

It sounds a bit technical, but there are many wearable devices on the market today that can give you feedback on your heart rate, body temperature, and even blood oxygen concentration. The FDA has approved biofeedback techniques, so if you are interested in learning more, you can talk to your doctor.

Activities like dancing and yoga make a noticeable difference in how you pay more attention to the physical and emotional signals from your mind and body, but exercise is absolutely essential for your well-being.

STRATEGY #6: PHYSICAL ACTIVITY

You don't have to be a gym junkie to appreciate the effects physical activity can have on you, physically and mentally.

A brisk walk is enough to increase the heart rate and manage the levels of stress hormones. Engaging in physical activity lowers cortisol and epinephrine, putting you in a better position to handle stress.

For overthinkers, physical activity isn't just about handling stress. It's a time when you can use movement to escape from the cycle of thoughts by challenging the brain through coordination, and the extra blood flow and oxygen to the brain helps with cognitive reasoning.

This strategy looks at ways you can incorporate more physical activity into your life, regardless of your current fitness levels.

No Exercise Physical Activity

You don't need to get your gym kit on in order to increase your physical activity. It's really a case of "every little helps."

Start by parking your car a little further away from where you need to be. Get off the bus or metro a stop earlier. Take the stairs instead of the elevator. Put some music on while you are cleaning, and add some dancing.

If your work requires a lot of sitting, try standing up while you are on phone calls, and instead of emailing or messaging coworkers, walk over to their desks. You can also encourage others to be more active with you by having standing meetings or leaving the office for short walks during breaks.

Wherever you are, try to include some basic stretches throughout the day to release pent-up tension.

Brisk Walking

Brisk walking doesn't sound like much, but as long as the heart rate is slightly increased, it counts toward the 150 minutes of recommended weekly exercise (Centers for Disease Control and Prevention, n.d.). Walking releases endorphins, which not only help to ease an overactive nervous system but also act as a natural painkiller.

One study has shown that fast walking can add years to your life. The extensive research included 475,000 people with varying weights and BMI (Body Mass Index). Those who walked faster added between 15 and 20 years to their life (Losinski, 2019). When you combine your walk with nature, you can further reduce your stress levels.

If you aren't a fan of walking, there are ways that can make it more fun. You can listen to audiobooks on Audible or your favorite podcast while walking.

Using a pedometer is a great way to start setting yourself attainable goals. Speaking of goals, if 30 minutes overwhelms you, start by setting a timer for 10 minutes and gradually adding on to this because it will get more enjoyable. You could even aim for 10 minutes two or three times a day.

Jogging

As you would imagine, jogging provides many of the same advantages as brisk walking but with more significant rewards. Stress is easier to handle, and heart health is boosted. Jogging can also improve brain power because new cells are created that help with decision-making, learning, and creativity. It can give you higher energy levels, motivating you to be more productive.

Sadly, there is still no cure for Alzheimer's, but jogging may help slow down cognitive decline by boosting the production of chemicals in the brain that keep the hippocampus healthy, an area crucial for memory and learning.

To start jogging, the best advice is to start walking, then turn walking into brisk walking, and then add short bursts of jogging.

For example, you may want to walk for 2 minutes and run for 30 seconds, which can soon turn into a 1-minute walk and a 1-minute jog. Before you know it, you will jog for 5 minutes and walk for 1 until you no longer need to walk. Always listen to your body. It's not about running fast. It's about running so that you are pushing your body but not causing yourself to suffer.

Swimming

Swimming offers a full-body workout, so heart health is improved as well as muscle strength. If you are looking to burn extra calories and fat, swimming is a great option. For instance, a person weighing 155 pounds can burn 432 calories an hour in the pool, compared with an average of 266 calories while brisk walking (Asp, 2022).

At the same time, it doesn't put as much strain on the body as jogging might, especially on the knees! For people with chronic pain conditions such as fibromyalgia, aquatic sports can improve physical function.

For the busy mind, I find swimming to be cleansing. It's actually a time when it's easier to remember fond memories from the past, especially childhood memories.

Many can remember happy times in a pool or at a beach splashing in water. Even the smell of the changing rooms helps me to think of happier times. Whether it's the smell of chlorine or the sensation of cold water on your skin, your senses will be engaged during your swim.

Apart from swimming, you can also try aquatic walking or aqua aerobics. Many aquatic centers will often offer both low-impact and high-impact sessions. You might be able to find deep water running and aqua Zumba too.

Strength Training

As well as 150 minutes of moderate-intensity physical activity, the Centers for Diseases and Prevention (CDC) also recommends two sessions of strength training a week.

Examples of strength training include weights, resistance bands, Pilates, and yoga. Wall Pilates is a popular trend because using a wall with stretching exercises increases resistance; essentially, your own body weight makes the workout more intense.

Most research has focused on how aerobic activities improve the symptoms of anxiety, stress, and depression, but the benefit of strength training for mental health is gaining interest. Research has shown how one-off and long-term training can have anxiolytic effects (anxiolytics are medications used to treat anxiety), regardless of gender or age (Strickland & Smith, 2014).

Here are some simple, no-equipment strength training exercises to get you started!

Squats

Stand with your feet a little wider than your hips. Push your chest out, but keep your shoulders back. Raise your arms in front of you, tighten your abs, and as you look straight ahead, lower your bottom to the ground, making sure that your knees don't extend out over your toes.

Your weight should remain in your heels, not your toes. As you return to the original position, gradually round your back to straighten the spin. Repeat the squat 15 to 20 times.

Plank

I have never really liked push-ups but can handle the plank, although it was only for 5 or 6 seconds at first. Begin on your hands and knees, and straighten your legs so that your weight is on your toes.

Next, lift your upper body off the ground so that you are in the starting position for a push-up. Keep your stomach pulled in so that your core is engaged. Hold the position for as long as you can, working toward the goal of 1 minute.

Glute Bridges

Your glutes are the most significant set of muscles in your body, and if they are strong, you can reduce the risk of injuries and back pain. Lay down with the heels of your feet flat on the floor. Keep your arms by your side. Squeeze your butt cheeks together and then raise your butt off the ground.

You want to imagine your body in a straight line from your knees to your shoulders. Roll your back down until your body is back on the ground. Repeat the bridge 15 to 20 times.

Biceps and Triceps

With your elbows tucked into your sides, bend your arms so that your elbows are at a 90-degree angle and your wrists are facing upwards. Lift your forearms, bringing your hands toward your shoulders. For a tricep kick, bend forward and put your elbows at a 90-degree angle again.

Next, straighten your arms out behind you. Both of these exercises can be done with weights or bottles of water for more resistance, but remember that the muscles need to do the work, not the momentum of swinging.

Cross Body Crunches

Lie on the floor with your feet flat and your fingers touching the back of your head. The fingers are there for support, and you shouldn't be using your arms to pull your head up. Lift the left leg and bring your right elbow across to touch your left inner knee. Repeat on the other side. You can aim to do 10 crunches on each side.

Physical Activity for the Introvert

It's perfectly understandable why you don't have it in you to join a gym or head to a park and exercise in front of others. It's not just the risk of introverts having to talk to others. Overthinkers can find that anxiety is enough to prevent them from venturing out to exercise. If this is the case, you can do so many workouts at home thanks to apps.

I don't like promoting any particular product, but I have had lots of success and fun with the FitOn app. There are hundreds of free workouts, including cardio, self-defense, boxing, yoga, and even meditation. Workouts can be as short as 5 minutes, and you can choose varying intensities.

Best of all, many of the instructors are "regular" people who don't make you feel less confident about your own shape, and there is a strong emphasis on protecting your mental health!

Don't make the common mistake that many do and overexert the body. Starting with short periods and building on them will make an exercise routine more enjoyable and easier to stick to. Choose activities that you are going to genuinely like, not things you think you should do.

I confess I am not a jogger. In fact, I hate it. I used to think that going for a jog was the adult thing to do, but because I didn't enjoy it, I never had the motivation to do it. On the other hand, although I had no idea what I was doing, I felt great after 15 minutes of Zumba and was keen to do the same the next day.

Ideas to Incorporate Physical Activity into Your Day for Lasting Impact

With so many different lifestyles, it's wrong to assume that everyone is in the same position to just start exercising, but there are still ways to increase your physical activity levels. Use the following list as ideas for inspiration and adapt any to suit your daily schedule.

• Find out if your workplace has an onsite gym

• Replace your chair with an exercise ball

- Walk around the building

- Eat lunch away from your desk

- Cycle to work or walk part of the way

- Switch Zoom calls for face-to-face visits

- Practice chair yoga at your desk

- Volunteer to walk your neighbor's dog

- Skip rope or have fun with a hula hoop

- Set up circuits in your home with different strength training workouts at each station

- Join a team sport

- Dance as you clean

- Do squats as you clean your teeth

What's Stopping You?

There will always be obstacles in our way that stop us from exercising. Fortunately, once you are into a new routine, these obstacles become few and far between. Nevertheless, the strategies below will help break down barriers to physical activity.

- Always keep a pair of trainers and exercise clothes in your car or workplace so you don't have to go home to change.

- Choose activities that don't require any equipment, so you aren't tied to a certain location.

- If you are unsure, talk to your doctor about the best types of exercise for you rather than putting it off.

- Don't use work as an excuse. Many hours will require your computer, but for all the rest, phone calls and even meetings can be done while you are walking.

- Cook in bulk so that meals are already prepared. You can easily save yourself 20 minutes a day!

- Get your kids involved with physical activities. Kick a ball around the park with them or through a frisbee. You will reap more rewards than just exercise.

- Set fitness goals with your partner and explore new activities that you both enjoy.

- For young children, look at activities that can be done together. For example, there are many yoga positions that are suitable with babies. Wear a baby carrier as you clean, or try fun baby and dad dancing classes!

- Stop comparing yourself to others, as this will impact your confidence. Everyone is on their own journey, and the most important thing is that you start your own!

Finally, take advantage of your best times of the day because trying to exercise when you are low on energy is hard work. For me, the mornings are a better time to find half an hour for myself because the children are still sleeping. And in the evenings, there is the usual list of tasks that need to be done.

Mornings might not be your best time, but when you get home from work, a quick workout can recharge you to make the most of the evening.

All of these steps will help you develop an exercise routine that is simple to integrate into your daily routine and something you are more likely to build on.

STRATEGY #7: BREATHWORK

Wellness, the mind-body connection, and physical activity wouldn't be complete without the amazing power of breathwork!

It may not come as a surprise now, but the brain associates different emotions with different types of breathing.

When the body is in a calm, relaxed state, breathing is regular. When we are stressed, anxious, or scared, breathing becomes faster and shallower.

Breathwork can trick the brain into thinking you are calm in moments when overthinking isn't providing any real threat or danger.

4-8-7 Breathing

Taking a deep breath isn't enough. Inhaling is linked to your fight-or-flight response. You need more oxygen in times of danger!

Inhaling too many times or too quickly may cause hyperventilation. On the other hand, exhaling is linked to the rest and digest response (when the body is in a calm state).

The 4-8-7 method involves breathing in for 4 seconds, holding it for 8 seconds, and breathing out for 7 seconds. In reality, it doesn't have to be 4-8-7, just as long as the exhale is longer than the inhale.

Lion's Breath

This is another technique that puts more emphasis on the exhale rather than the inhale. Sit comfortably but without slouching. Rest your hands on your lap or your knees. Inhale, and as you exhale, stick your tongue out and extend your chin as far as you can. Force the breath out as you make a "ha" sound.

Belly Breathing

Also known as diaphragmatic breathing, belly breathing engages the muscles just below the lungs, and regular practice can make breathing easier on the body. You can sit or lie down, whichever is more comfortable. Place one hand on your heart and the other above your belly button. As you inhale through your nose, pay attention to how your chest and stomach move.

Can you control your breathing so that the chest moves more than the stomach or the stomach more than the chest?

Alternative Nostril Breathing

In a Yogic breathing practice, the right nostril is associated with higher levels of arousal, and the left nostril is associated with reduced stress. You can achieve balance using both nostrils.

Press your left thumb on your left nostril and inhale through the right nostril. With the left ring finger, pinch the left nostril and release your left thumb to exhale through the left nostril. Of course, if it's more comfortable, you can do this the opposite way around by using your right hand.

All of these breathwork techniques take only a couple of minutes, making them perfect to incorporate many times during the day. Instead of rushing out of bed in the mornings, take a moment to breathe!

Before you fall asleep, try a different technique. Set alarms on your phone as reminders or start a new habit of practicing deep breathing before each tea or coffee you make or meal/snack you have. The benefits will surprise you in a short time!

This chapter has covered the importance of taking care of your physical self to mitigate the effects of stress, anxiety, and depression caused by overthinking.

They are ways to begin healing on the inside and outside, and they are crucial coping techniques that will help with the next chapter, which takes a deeper dive into how we can unravel the negativity that consumes us!

CHAPTER THREE: I: INNER STRENGTH

 You need a negative focus to survive, but a positive one to thrive.

DR. RICHARD BOYATZIS

When we discussed cognitive distortions, we briefly mentioned the negativity bias, but it's worth exploring this psychological phenomenon in more detail to understand how real and powerful it is!

Imagine you are at a party, and 10 people come up to you and mention how fantastic you look, but one person says that your hair is out of place. Why is it that you will spend hours, if not days, dwelling on the one negative comment rather than all of the nice things that others said?

Before science and technology were better able to understand this, you would have been labeled a neg-head. Neuroscientists measured the event-related brain potentials (ERPs) of participants when shown positive, negative, and neutral stimuli. The results showed that negative stimuli caused more electrical activity in the cerebral cortex than neutral and positive stimuli (Larsen et al., 1998).

The consequences of the negativity bias can greatly impact lives. When watching or reading the news, we are more likely to believe the bad news because it calls more attention and seems more valid. This can even have an effect on our political beliefs.

In relationships, we are more inclined to think and expect the worst in others. Even before this, our negative first impressions of someone can be created based on the opinions of others. Although they provide a balance of positive and negative adjectives, we pay more attention to the negative.

As hardwired as you might think your brain is, rewiring is possible!

STRATEGY #8: ESCAPING THE NEGATIVITY TRAP

It's a bit of a chicken or egg situation. Is your overthinking caused by your brain's tendency to lean to the negative, which fuels cognitive distortions, or do your cognitive distortions stoke the negativity bias? On top of these two factors, there is another bias: the confirmation bias.

Confirmation bias is the subconscious habit of focusing on and giving more credit to things that fit with our existing beliefs.

A simple example is that we see someone wearing glasses, and we assume that this person reads a lot and is intelligent.

In a sports game, if the referee makes a decision that is in favor of our team, it's the right decision. However, if it goes against the team, it's the wrong decision.

Horoscopes are a classic example. The information is so vague and interpretive that we choose to interpret and believe what suits our own perspective. It's not intentional, so please don't beat yourself up about it!

There are three main types of confirmation bias:

• **Biased attention:** When we focus on information that confirms our views, but at the same time, we discount or ignore anything that doesn't fit.

• **Biased interpretation:** It's a conscious act where information is interpreted in a way that confirms beliefs.

• **Biased memory:** We remember specific information that aligns with our views while discounting or ignoring what doesn't fit.

There are consequences to this bias, too. It can influence your decisions because choices could be made after giving more credit to the information that aligns with your beliefs. It's harder to process information rationally and in an unbiased way when an opinion has already been formed.

It can also impact relationships and the relationships you form. It's easier to make friends with people who are more likely to agree with you and your beliefs. This is not always the best foundation for a relationship.

All of these biases lead you to get stuck in a giant negative trap that is impossible to escape. After all, if the brain is physically wired this way, can it really be changed?

In the past, it was believed that once we reached a certain age, our brains stopped developing. Fortunately, since the late 1940s, research on neuroplasticity has developed, and we now understand that we can change the brain's structure—and I'm not talking about drugs or surgery.

The brain contains billions of cells called neurons, approximately 86 billion in total. A thought is created when a neuron fires up and sends electrical signals to nearby neurons thanks to chemicals known as neurotransmitters. The connection made between the neurons is called a synapse or neural pathway.

Imagine learning any new information. Every time you repeat the information, the neurons that created the original neural pathway fire up again, and the connection strengthens. In the end, the information or action is repeated so often that it becomes second nature, even automatic.

It's like driving a car. After years behind the wheel, you don't need to think about it in the same way as you did when you were learning because the neural pathways are so strong.

Consider a hobby that you used to do as a child. If you haven't practiced it in a while and it's not repeated, the connection between the neurons may have weakened, making you feel like a complete novice again. The same concept can be applied to overthinking and negative thoughts.

The more times you replay a negative thought, the stronger the connection becomes. However, you also know that it's not as simple as forgetting your childhood hobby.

To escape the negativity trap, the brain needs new neural pathways!

This is where positive affirmations come in. Positive affirmations are short phrases repeated, often in sets and at different times of the day. The more often these affirmations are repeated, the more often the neurons are fired up and wired together. Eventually, the neural pathways that were once racing with negative thoughts diminish, and the positive affirmations are easier to recall.

Some examples of positive affirmations include:

- I am in complete control of my thoughts and feelings

- I am free from anxiety and worry

- I have the power to choose my thoughts

- I enjoy a clear mind

- I am safe, and my life is in my hands

- Things are less scary than my mind makes them out to be

- I am stronger than my constructive thoughts

- My best is good enough

- My mind is at peace at the moment

- I will focus on what makes me happy

- I can switch off my thoughts at will

It's important that the affirmation you use has meaning. The brain has to believe what you are telling it, so if the words make you feel silly or sound cheesy, they won't be effective. You can also create your own affirmations. Just make sure they are in the present tense and don't contain any negative words or contractions.

Positive affirmations are a great companion for gradual exposure. Some of the hardest negativity traps come from fear. If you have to give a presentation in front of a dozen people, you may find yourself starting to experience negative thoughts even weeks before the event.

Gradual exposure therapy is a type of therapy used in dialectical behavioral therapy (DBT) and is particularly beneficial for overcoming fears. By gradually exposing yourself to the fear, the emotional response slowly decreases.

Take the example of the presentation. Instead of spending the weeks leading up to the presentation working yourself up into a mess, you can break down the fear into smaller, manageable steps.

The first would be practicing the presentation by yourself. Once you are comfortable, do the presentation in front of a mirror. Keep practicing in the mirror until you are emotionally comfortable. Next, you can give the presentation to a friend, then two friends, and so on. It's crucial not to rush to the next stage until you stop reacting to the fear.

STRATEGY #9: EMOTIONAL FORTITUDE

Each thought, emotion, and action are linked. An idea is something that we are consciously aware of in our minds. Emotions are subconscious feelings that come from thoughts, and many of our actions are based on our emotions. A person who lacks emotional intelligence is unable to control the triangle, and without intervention, it's impossible to stop.

Emotional intelligence is the ability to recognize, manage, and use your own emotions as well as recognize and even influence the emotions of others. That's not to say that you use this skill to manipulate others. It can be as simple as smiling at someone and encouraging them to smile back, improving their day.

There are five fundamental elements of emotional intelligence: self-regulation, social skills, empathy, motivation, and self-awareness.

Self-awareness is the key to overthinking. By increasing emotional intelligence, you can increase self-reflection and self-analysis. If you are thinking that this sounds exactly like overthinking, it's not the case. Overthinking serves no purpose. Self-awareness is a chance to process thoughts and feelings. With self-awareness, you are in control, whereas overthinking controls you.

Emotional intelligence has a wealth of benefits. Managing your own emotions can prevent them from taking over a situation and you from reacting rather than responding. In turn, this helps with all relationships, professional and personal, especially when dealing with conflict.

Increasing empathy also strengthens relationships and connections, though this is typically an area of emotional intelligence that overthinkers are pretty skilled in. So much time spent thinking has provided plenty of opportunities to imagine how others are feeling.

For the workplace, emotional intelligence improves communication skills, and combined with empathy, this makes for better leaders. Morale, motivation, and productivity are increased, and research has shown that those with a higher level of emotional intelligence can earn an average of $29,000 more a year than those with low emotional intelligence (Bradberry, 2014).

The focus of this strategy is how to develop greater self-awareness to reduce the effects and manage overthinking. Here are ways you can increase your self-awareness.

Label Emotions Accurately

If you have a habit of answering "I'm fine" to everything, stop this. It's normal not to go around telling everyone that you are anxious, afraid, hurt, or angry, as you don't want to come across as negative. At the same time, you may avoid announcing feelings like happiness, excitement, joy, or eagerness because others may not feel so positive. But you are entitled to feel your emotions and express them, especially when asked.

Even when not being asked, please take a moment to explore your emotions and label them more accurately. On the surface, you may feel sad, but is that because you are bored, tired, pressured, or feeling out of control?

Keep a Daily Journal for Self-Reflection

Ask yourself questions like:

• What meaningful things happened in my day today?

• What were the highs and lows of my day?

- Which emotions were most dominant throughout the day?

- How did I react to those emotions?

- Were others affected by my emotions?

- Which situations could I have handled better today?

This doesn't have to take a long time. Much like wellness integration, 5 minutes is a great place to start. If you aren't keen on writing, you can keep a video diary or even just take a few mindful moments to think about the responses.

Ask for Feedback

Feedback for an overthinker can be challenging because it's literally fuel for your thoughts. Before asking for feedback, make sure you are mentally prepared. You need to go in with an attitude that doesn't turn into defensiveness. Remind yourself that this is a learning experience that is a vital part of your self-awareness journey.

The person you ask for feedback from has to be someone you trust and someone you know will be honest. As much as you want to hear all positive things, it may not be the most productive conversation.

At the same time, don't just ask questions that will lead to areas of improvement. If you are going to ask, "When am I at my worst?" you should also be asking, "When am I at my best?"

Get to Know Your Personal Values

Your behaviors and actions are based on your personal values. These personal values determine the way you work and live, and they guide your decisions and affect the way you treat others. Essentially, they are the things that matter to you, such as kindness, perseverance, loyalty, and respect.

Look at people you know and consider what their personal values are. You can even find inspiration from fictional characters. Write a list of your personal values and then organize them so that your priorities are at the top. Which of these values do you find yourself spending the most or least energy on, and is this in line with your priorities?

As you become more aware of your triggers, you will know what things cause stress, anxiety, and fear. It's natural to want to avoid them, but there will eventually be a situation that is unavoidable. At the same time, with strength, overcoming these types of situations can improve the way you handle emotions in difficult times and allow for personal growth.

Exposure therapy is often therapist-led but can be done yourself or with a trusted friend or family member if you need additional support. The idea is to define the cause of your emotional reaction and gradually expose yourself to it.

Let's say you have a fear of heights to the extent that you overthink each day, wondering how you will cope with driving over a bridge, the stairs you have to climb, or the view from a window in a high-rise building.

Exposure therapy would break down the steps, repeating each gentle exposure until there is no emotional reaction. In the case of heights, you would start by looking at images of heights until you can look at an image without your heart racing. The next step might be parking your car on the second level of a multi-story car parking lot and remaining at this stage until there is no emotional response.

It might take a while to overcome the stress and fear, but if you can master your emotions in these situations, there is very little that you can't handle!

STRATEGY #10: BUILDING EMOTIONAL RESILIENCE

We do need to be realistic! While you will be able to master your overthinking, it's very unlikely that all causes of stress and anxiety are just going to disappear.

Emotional intelligence will help you manage your feelings, but emotional resilience will improve your ability to handle stressful situations and unexpected crises. Even those who are more sensitive to difficult situations can develop this skill.

The word "resilience" comes from the Latin "resilio" meaning "to bounce back". It's a two-way street. Emotional intelligence helps with emotional resilience and vice versa. But it also reduces the risk of mental health conditions and engaging in high-risk behaviors.

Excessive drinking and substance abuse are often used as coping mechanisms in times of stress. Another benefit of emotional resilience is stronger social ties and long-term relationships.

A major part of emotional resilience is emotional fortitude, the ability to keep going when facing intense emotions such as disappointment or confronting fears. It enables you to cope with the emotions that arise from challenges and allows you to see how you can learn from them. Above all, it reduces the risk of mental health conditions such as anxiety and depression.

If you need an amazing example of emotional fortitude, look no further than Malala Yousafzai. Malala was an activist for girls' education in Pakistan. Even after receiving death threats, she continued to fight for what she believed in. On October 9, 2012, a Pakistani Taliban boarded a bus she was on and shot her through the head. Miraculously, she survived, but it was her emotional fortitude that enabled her to go on and become the world's youngest Nobel Prize winner for her fight against the suppression of children's rights to education.

The beauty of emotional fortitude is that everything you put into practice in this strategy, as well as the others, will help you strengthen this skill. Here are some of the traits and practices that foster emotional fortitude:

- Resilience

- Emotional regulation

- Self-awareness

- Mindfulness

- Adaptability

- Self-care

- Journaling

- Positive affirmations

- Meditation

Developing Flexibility

One of the keys to achieving emotional resilience is to become more flexible. Mindfulness will help with this because it's much-needed time spent in the present because you are more able to handle situations the right way.

When a car cuts you off while you are lost in thought, it can spark an inappropriate reaction. Mindfulness in this situation keeps your focus on the road and everything going on around you. You may even have noticed the signs of the car about to cut you off before it happened!

Flexibility also requires accepting the things you can't change and even the things that you are not responsible for, including the emotional response and actions of others.

If there is one thing the pandemic taught us, it is the art of flexibility. Some things are simply out of our hands, and fighting against it only causes emotional turmoil.

Cognitive flexibility also plays a role in resilience. There is always going to be more than one way to handle a stressful situation. If you have the ability to take a step back and attempt to see things from different perspectives, your cognitive flexibility will allow you to switch from one coping strategy to another, depending on the situation.

Another way to see things from different perspectives is to surround yourself with people who are emotionally resilient.

We all know someone who seems to take things in their stride. Walt Disney is one of my favorite examples. He was fired from his first job because he wasn't creative enough. And that was his first setback of many.

Building Your Support System

And while on the subject of those around you, your ability to bounce back from the harder times can be made much easier when you have a solid support system.

Remember, it's the quality, not the quantity, of trusted ones who will help you through the challenges. That's not to say that a good social circle isn't nice. But the 1,000 followers on social media can't compare to the handful of people in your life who would drop anything to be by your side!

Many people will turn to spirituality to build their support system. Religion can significantly help overcome tragedy. You don't need to be religious to appreciate the power of a religious community, and you don't need to be religious to practice spirituality.

Spirituality can be very individual. Some may find it during mind-body practices, others in solitude (the time when you choose to be alone because it's what you want and need), and others in nature.

Defining Your Values and Morals

Previously, we learned how values can increase your self-awareness, but your morals and values can also help you find meaning in your actions. Considering you spend a significant number of hours at work, this is the ideal place to start. Take a moment to reflect and realize that, in some way, the work you do is helping someone!

If you can't find meaning in your work, there will be a way to find meaning in other areas of life. You could try volunteering, donating to a cause, even if it's your time, or becoming a mentor.

When you look at the bigger picture, what you do matters, and you have a positive impact on others. When times are hard, knowing this can drive you forward.

Enjoy a Laugh

Don't forget the power of laughter. Those who are highly resilient can experience positive emotions with the help of humor, even during times of stress. This doesn't mean you aren't taking a matter seriously; it's about putting things back in perspective.

Imagine giving a presentation. Nerves get the better of you, and your words don't come out right. You have two options: retreat in shame or embarrassment or laugh about it.

Neither shame nor laughter means you don't know your subject matter! However, choosing to laugh can help dissolve the uncomfortable emotions you experience and improve connections with others, considering laughter is contagious.

Learn From Your Challenges

Now that you are aware of the negativity bias, it's easier to take a step back, recognize this thought pattern, and see past and present challenges from a different perspective.

If you didn't get a job, it's not all bad. You can review the interview, make necessary changes, and even get a job that would actually better suit your needs.

This is possible if you can see the opportunities that challenges present. To achieve this, follow these steps:

Step 1: Focus only on the facts and ask yourself what happened.

Step 2: Recognize the emotions that the challenge creates.

Step 3: Take responsibility for your part in what happened so you don't fall into the habit of a victim mentality.

Step 4: Consider how you view the situation and whether this view serves your highest purpose.

Step 5: Once you remove the pain you are experiencing, what lesson can you take from the challenge or situation?

Step 6: Visualize yourself in the same situation, but now apply the lesson you learned. Imagine the positive outcome.

Step 7: Apply this lesson to all applicable areas in your life, and don't just wait for the next challenge.

Finally, between the flexibility and a dash of humor, remember to be kind to yourself. Whether it's a stressful situation or a change you find hard to adapt to, it can be draining. You deserve and need a break from the usual routine to recharge your batteries.

STRATEGY #11: COGNITIVE RESTRUCTURING PRACTICES

When talking to trauma survivors, special forces instructors, and prisoners of war, Steven Southwick and Dennis Charney noticed that those who have witnessed horrendous experiences have a particular trait in common. They are all optimistic, and this helps with their emotional resilience. But this can't be forced.

How many times have you heard someone say, "Just look on the bright side" or "Every day is a day to be happy"?

In their own way, they are only trying to help, but these recycled words of so-called wisdom are known as toxic positivity. It involves pressuring you to think only positive thoughts, and as a result, you end up feeling worse about negative thoughts and perceived negative emotions. These thoughts and emotions then get suppressed.

Buried doesn't mean they are resolved! More likely than not, these thoughts and feelings only reappear at another point and are stronger than they were before.

Negative thoughts are real and destructive, but each emotion is there to serve a purpose and shouldn't be viewed as solely negative. Remember that you have the right to feel each and every emotion, and it's far healthier to work through these emotions than telling yourself just to stay positive.

Toxic positivity can also apply to negative thoughts. Imagine telling yourself that you are a failure and can't get anything right. How helpful is it to end that sentence with "It could be worse"? It's completely unhelpful. Instead, it's essential to break the sentence down and rephrase it so that it's both positive and reflective of the truth.

Cognitive restructuring is an important part of cognitive behavioral therapy (CBT). CBT helps people to identify negative or unhealthy thoughts and thought patterns, interrupt them, and then reframe them so that they are more accurate. Learning this skill can reduce stress and anxiety, replace unhealthy coping mechanisms, and boost confidence and self-esteem.

One method of cognitive reconstructing is the Socratic approach. Socrates developed the method as a way for teachers and students to explore underlying beliefs that contribute to a student's way of thinking. The Socratic method involves a series of questions. The person answers each question incorrectly (at least unrealistically) until they are able to provide solid evidence to the contrary.

Let's look at an example.

• What are you worried about?

- Arguing with a family member at an upcoming event.

• What do you think will happen?

- My parents will be angry because I should know better.

• What will you do if this happens?

- Feel embarrassed and most likely distance myself from my family.

• What assumptions are you making?

- That there will be an argument in the first place.

• Is there an alternative outcome?

- We could all go on family occasions and have a good time.

Next, we will go through a more detailed cognitive reconstruction approach.

Step 1: Take a moment to calm down

One of my all-time favorite quotes comes from Viktor Frankl, who survived the Holocaust but sadly lost most of his family members while in different concentration camps. "Between stimulus and response, there is a space. In that space is our power to choose our response. In our response lies our growth and our freedom."

The space between what causes our negative thoughts and the reaction that follows might be just a split second, but it's always there. It will take a little practice to take advantage of this space, but even a couple of deep breaths can make all the difference.

Step 2: Find the trigger

Though we covered this in the first chapter, don't forget to take some time to get to the real bottom of your trigger. More often than not, by asking yourself what had happened before and then before that, you will see that it may not be something that someone else said or did but your own thoughts that triggered you.

Step 3: What's your mood?

There is no doubt that your mood influences your thoughts. Try to step aside from the emotions surrounding a thought, analyze the mood you are in, and decide if this is fueling the thoughts. For example, you probably know that you will react differently to a thought when you are tired or hungry compared to when you are relaxed.

Step 4: Identify your automatic negative thoughts (ANTs).

Many situations can lead to the same thought automatically popping into your head. For instance, you can stall your car in front of the police controlling traffic, or you can send an email and forget the attachments, or you can have an argument with your partner, and the first thing you think each time is "I'm such an idiot!"

66

Step 5: Find evidence to support the ANTs

If you tell yourself you are an idiot, what evidence do you have to back that up? Can you really call yourself stupid?

Regardless of where you are in life, there will be more evidence to the contrary, whether that's qualifications, financial security, you are raising children, or you are learning new skills (just as you are now). Be objective. Answer this question as if you were talking to a friend.

Step 5: Consider if there is any truth behind the ANTs

There is a massive difference between an act of stupidity and being stupid. Everyone makes mistakes, and taking responsibility for them is important, but the ANT is rarely justified!

Step 6: Rephrase your negative thought

From our above example, the steps have shown us that the original thought is untrue, and there is evidence to support the fact that you aren't an idiot, but at the same time, a mistake was made. In this situation, a more helpful thought would be, "I made a mistake, it wasn't the end of the world, and I can learn from it." You will see there is no sugarcoating or toxic positivity, just an honest statement that is beneficial and compassionate.

It's good to get into the habit of combining cognitive reconstructing with other practices that contribute to better mental health. In some cases, you will use these steps at the moment when negative thoughts start to intrude on your daily activities, but other times, you will carve out time to process thoughts that need a little extra time.

Try taking a few minutes for mindfulness, followed by using your journal to work through the process. After writing, practice mindfulness again to notice how the mind is calmer.

Journal Prompts for Cognitive Restructuring

Use the following journal prompts. It's a good idea to repeat the questions as you face different types of challenges and negative thoughts so that you gain more self-awareness:

• What is the one thing you wish you could change about your thinking patterns?

• What is one fear you have? Where is the evidence to support that fear?

• Name one thing you did today that made you feel anxious or scared.

• What is the first negative thought about yourself that comes to mind? Challenge it!

• Describe how a recent negative thought has impacted your behavior.

• Describe how a recent negative thought has influenced a decision you made.

• Write about a negative thought you have had that turned out to be unjustified.

• Identify an irrational belief you had today.

• Write a conversation between your rational and irrational self.

- What irrational beliefs or negative thoughts do you have about the future? How can you overcome these thoughts?

Mindful Meditation

If you need a little extra help with cognitive reconstruction and negative thoughts (and this is perfectly normal), guided meditations are great for keeping your focus on a voice so that the mind doesn't start to take over. Here are some guided meditations that have helped me.

Working with Difficult Thoughts: Meditation

Picture your growing inner strength as the foundation for the next level. As overthinking becomes less of an issue, there is more mental space for other activities that will further subside the mental chatter. You might not believe it, but deep down inside, you have a creative side that is bursting to show you the joys of life.

Controlling Negative Thoughts: Meditation

CHAPTER FOUR: T: TRANSFORMATIVE CREATIVITY

 Perhaps imagination is only intelligence having fun.

GEORGE SCIAI ARRA

I blame adulthood and perfectionism for the lack of creativity in our lives. As children, we would happily create all types of projects and be proud of our efforts. The disappointment of expectations versus reality quickly stops us from practicing any form of creativity, and this is such a shame considering the connection between imagination, anxiety, and intelligence.

Ironically, this one practice that can help your overthinking may also be the cause of it! The same thing that fuels your anxiety is what enables incredible creativity, and that is your imagination. Edvard Munch's *The Scream* came to him as a vision of himself trembling with anxiety. He recognized that his art would never have been the same without his extreme fear of life.

The link between anxiety and creativity has fascinated scientists. Studies have shown that writers are 121 percent more likely to suffer from bipolar disorder than those in non-creative jobs (ParentCo, 2022). Bipolar and anxiety disorders are the most common comorbidity!

The reason for this correlation is the way the brain works. Creativity and mental health conditions cause the brain to create visions before something happens. These visions can become works of art or negative thoughts to ruminate on. In this chapter, we will explore how creativity can be an effective outlet for anxiety and overthinking by reversing this process.

STRATEGY #12: LEVERAGING CREATIVITY FOR COGNITIVE FLEXIBILITY

Remember that cognitive flexibility enables you to switch your perspective and the way you think. Creativity is a fun way to improve cognitive flexibility and transform your thought patterns. Here are just some of the benefits of creativity:

• It engages the mind, allowing information to be more easily absorbed and appreciate non-linear thinking.

• It can improve communication by expressing thoughts and emotions when the right words can't be found.

• It can tap into different learning styles and cultures with an open mind.

• It allows for better problem-solving and innovation.

- It encourages questions, curiosity, reflection, and motivation.

- It can help you find your purpose and meaning, making interaction more fulfilling.

According to neuroscience professor Arne Dietrich, there are four types of creativity.

Type 1: Deliberate and Cognitive Creativity

People prefer experiments and investigations. They have high levels of concentration and find creativity in gathering information.

Type 2: Deliberate and Emotional Creativity

It combines logic and facts with emotional sensitivity. Times of quiet allow this creative type to have moments of both clarity and inspiration.

Type 3: Spontaneous and Cognitive Creativity

This requires a change of activity for a person to find their creativity. Rather than focusing on the problem at hand, engaging in different activities activates their unconscious awareness, giving them external inspiration.

Type 4: Spontaneous and Emotional Creativity

It occurs when the amygdala, the part of the brain that controls emotions, creates bursts of inspiration. These epiphanies allow people to see things from different points of view.

Being creative isn't just about being flexible in your thinking. According to the dual pathway to creativity model, it's a mix of two things: being able to think flexibly and not giving up easily, which is called cognitive persistence.

Cognitive persistence means that when you face a challenge, you keep looking for different ways to solve it instead of giving up. The model suggests that creativity gets a boost when you're in a good mood because it stimulates flexible thinking.

Interestingly, even when you're in a bad mood, creativity can increase because it stimulates persistence (Nijstad et al., 2010). You don't have to wait for a positive mood to tap into your creative side.

If you are worried about your creativity, you might be focused more on the artistic activities rather than the full scope of potential. Creativity can include music, woodwork, photography, gardening, dance, clay modeling, and baking.

If you doubt your creative skills, it's essential that you stop comparing your creations to those of others, especially not those from magazines, websites, and social media, because this is what can quickly turn a fun, creative activity into anxiety and overthinking!

When you suffer from a creativity block, and your persistence needs a helping hand, divergent thinking is the key to moving forward by looking at multiple solutions and perspectives.

A convergent thinker sees that the photocopier is broken and calls the technician. A divergent thinker may call the technician, but before, they would have to look online for a troubleshooting guide or send a group message to all co-workers to see if anyone knows the solution.

There will always be more than one way to solve a creative problem, and divergent thinkers are the best at finding the best solution because they can see things from more perspectives!

Here is a simple exercise to practice your divergent thinking skills, which can be done anywhere and any number of times. All you need is a timer, a pen and paper, and a random object. Set the timer and write down as many uses for that object as you can think of. There is no limit to the object's uses as long as you can explain it, so don't worry about going way out of the box.

For example, I have a mug in front of me. Apart from hot drinks, I can use it to make mug cakes, store pens, a small plant container, a candle holder, let my kids paint it, and so on.

When the 3 minutes are up, consider how quickly the ideas came to you and how diverse each one is. Are any of your ideas original? Make this a regular practice with various objects, and notice how your creativity starts to increase.

STRATEGY #13: ENCOURAGING PRESENT MOMENT FOCUS THROUGH CREATIVE FLOW

I can almost guarantee that every single case of your overthinking has been about the past or the future. Stress, anxiety, and depression are very much felt in the present moment, but the cause and triggers are from things that have happened or the fear of things that may happen. This is why being more present is important for breaking free from overthinking.

There is an ideal way to completely absorb yourself in creativity and the present moment through Mihaly Csikszentmihalyi's flow concept. Csikszentmihalyi, a psychologist, believed that the best moments are those when the body and mind are stretched to the limits while attempting to achieve something difficult and worthwhile. Flow is that moment when you are doing something and know that you are completely "in the zone"!

When the brain is in this state of flow, the prefrontal cortex is less active. This part of the brain is responsible for higher cognitive function, memory, and consciousness. Less activity in the prefrontal cortex can lead to a loss of self-consciousness, inhibiting the inner critic. Also, while this part of the brain is less active, other areas of the brain are more able to communicate with each other and engage in creativity.

Csikszentmihalyi's Flow Experience model shows the intricate link between a person's challenge, their skills, and levels of anxiety or boredom.

When the challenge matches our skills, we're in this incredible state called "flow," where everything just clicks. But if things get too tricky, stress can creep in, making it hard to keep up. On the flip side, if it's too easy, boredom sets in, and we start to lose interest.

So, the key is to aim for that "just right" level of challenge where we're fully engaged and having a blast.

How to find your flow

Take a moment to consider the last challenge you faced. Where would you rate your experience on the model?

Csikszentmihalyi identified eight characteristics of flow:

1. Complete concentration on the task
2. Clarity of goals and rewards in mind and immediate feedback
3. Transformation of time (speeding up or slowing down—time distortion)
4. The experience of intrinsically rewarding
5. Effortless and ease
6. A balance between challenge and skills
7. Actions and awareness are merged, losing self-conscious rumination
8. There is a feeling of control over the task (Oppland, 2016)

To find your flow, choose an activity you care about and are good at. The task you choose has to be something that isn't too difficult but not too easy. This is often referred to as the Goldilocks Effect, finding that "just right" balance between the two extremes.

To concentrate entirely on the task, you need to remove any distractions. For some people, this means turning their phone on silent mode. For others, it could mean making sure their surroundings are tidy or that there is peace and quiet.

Finally, keep in mind that the final reward should not be the creation but the journey. Rather than thinking about the delicious cake you can enjoy, pay attention to the progress you make as you add each ingredient. Instead of creating tangible rewards, flow is heightened when rewards are centered on personal growth, internal motivation, and a sense of accomplishment.

Here are some good activities to try to find your flow:

- Painting or drawing

- Scrapbooking or making a collage

- Reading a book

- Trying a balancing yoga pose

- Go on a nature adventure

- Take part in a sport

- Challenge yourself with a video game

- Take up calligraphy

- Start an e-learning course that excites you

Creativity and flow are perfect for improving emotional awareness in the present moment. Next, it's time to see how creativity can help express emotions.

STRATEGY #14: UTILIZING CREATIVE EXPRESSION TO PROCESS EMOTIONS

If you struggle to talk about your thoughts and feelings, and this is understandable if those around you have been less than supportive, expressive arts therapy can help interpret and describe how you feel, whether with a trained therapist or by yourself. Common types of expressive therapies include:

- **Music therapy:** playing instruments, listening to music, or singing

- **Art therapy:** painting, drawing, sculpting, self-portrait, finger painting

- **Dance therapy:** different types of movement to music

- **Drama therapy:** role play, voice work, storytelling, improvisation

- **Writing therapy:** journaling, writing stories, writing poetry, writing songs

- **Photo therapy:** using photos to evoke thoughts and feelings

- **Filmmaking:** recording and editing films or videos to explore emotions

It's possible that the concept of expressive art therapy conjures up images of a hippy movement, but the practices have plenty of research behind them. Studies have shown that art therapy has helped with the reduction of anxiety and depression symptoms, pain relief in patients with Alzheimer's disease, and improved communication in those with autism (Hu et al., 2021).

Overall, expressive therapy can significantly help reduce the symptoms of those suffering from a wide range of mental health conditions, neurodiverse conditions, and physical conditions while improving quality of life.

For expressive art therapy to have an effect, the only important thing to keep in mind when engaging in an activity is genuine self-expression. Self-expression is about communicating your true self, reflecting on your life, and releasing all the pent-up feelings you have suppressed for so long.

At the same time, self-expression can lead us to feel vulnerable. This might seem like a bad thing as we often feel that vulnerability is a weakness. Vulnerability means being susceptible to harm, but emotional vulnerability means being open to your emotional experiences and acknowledging uncomfortable or painful ones.

Expressing yourself through any form of art is a process that might be painful but with a sense of freedom on the other side. For this reason, it's not the same as simply painting a picture or writing a story. It's a process of self-discovery.

Here are some steps to increase your emotional expression through creativity.

• Talk about your day and how certain moments made you feel

• Use your body language to express your emotions

• Take photos of things that cause different emotions within you

• Use colors that reflect your emotions (red represents anger, yellow happiness, blue sadness, green calm, etc.)

• Make your day into a short movie by recording events and how they made you feel

• Build a quote wall with quotes that relate to your thoughts and feelings

• Release intense emotions through scribbling

- Practice symbolic release by writing about emotions, ripping the paper up, and throwing the pieces away

- Wear clothes that aren't necessarily fashionable but represent who you are

- Create an emotional playlist

For true self-expression, don't dance like nobody is watching. Dance because nobody is watching. Nobody is forming opinions of you. Nobody is scoring your efforts and, least of all, your results.

STRATEGY #15: CULTIVATING MINDFULNESS AND PRESENCE WITH CREATIVITY

Until now, we have seen mindfulness in the traditional sense of training the mind to focus on the present, an activity we can incorporate into daily lives.

Ellen Langer, one of the pioneers of mindfulness research, takes on another approach. Her approach is that life should be incorporated into mindfulness and meditation as a way of flicking off the autopilot switch and becoming aware of what we are doing.

If you go through life on autopilot, it's easy to miss out on reaching your full potential because you are just working your way through a process of steps and phases.

Look at it from a different point of view. If you are stuck on autopilot, you will look at every rose in the same way. You won't stop considering how each rose can differ, leading to thoughts based only on firsthand experiences. Creativity is a chance to fully immerse yourself in the present, discovering things often overlooked as the mind obsesses over the past and future.

Limiting yourself to firsthand experiences leads to another problem: assuming that past creativity failures mean future attempts will also fail or that you are no good at drawing, so you can't be creative! Being creative isn't about producing pieces for an exhibition!

Mindful Coloring

There are so many adult coloring books and images to download, and for good reason. Just watch a child get lost in their coloring! To practice mindful coloring, try using various media, from chalk to paints, even scented paints. Pay attention to how different media feel as you use them, the smell, and the color hues they produce.

Happiness Scrapbook

Remember that this is not the same as a photo album that includes past memories or a vision board that looks at future aspirations. Use magazines or internet images that represent things that make you happy in the present moment.

Recently, I saw a sugar packet that read, "Even if you feel like you don't have strength right now, don't give up." It made me happy, so it went into the scrapbook!

Sand Art

Sand art comes from the practice of sand mandala, where Buddhists use colored sand to make incredible pieces of art and then ritually destroy them, showing impermanence.

This is a type of therapy, but with a box, some sand, and even just a fork and spoon, it's easy to focus your attention on the patterns you can create.

Breath Drawing

With a large piece of paper and any media you feel like, take a deep breath in, and as you breathe out, draw what you feel. This could be wisps of lines, squiggles, or spirals. Experiment with longer breaths and even the pressure you use when drawing.

Leaf Printing

It's a classic activity for children but a great way to feel creative. Choose a range of different leaves, shapes, sizes, and vein patterns. Dip the veiny side of the leaf into the paint, wipe off the excess, and press the leaf onto a piece of paper. Notice the different prints caused by the leaves and break the mold using colors that aren't just associated with leaves.

Self-Portrait with Nature

When out for a walk, gather different objects (be mindful of what you pick up and avoid disrupting natural environments), such as pebbles, stones, twigs, leaves, shells from the beach, or seaweed, if permitted. Use these objects to make an abstract self-portrait.

Essential Oils Splatter Art

Choose a variety of colored paints. I find acrylic paints are better for their consistency. For each color, add a different essential oil. Dip a paintbrush into a paint and flick the paint onto paper or cardboard. The essential oils help create a sensory experience while flicking paint lets go of the need to paint something "perfect."

Mindful Rocks

Try to find flat, or at least smooth rocks. You can use leftover scented paints to decorate the rocks, but then choose a powerful and meaningful word to write on the rock in a permanent pen.

There is one more creative activity that strays from the traditional idea of creativity but definitely falls under making something of excellent value. Mindful gardening gives you the chance to grow your own food, even if it's just herbs to add to your dishes.

Scientists have discovered that soil contains a natural antidepressant, mycobacterium vaccae, that has similar effects on brain neurons to Prozac (Grant, 2023).

Mindful gardening can engage your hearing, touch, sight, and smell, and once you have grown even the easiest of plants, your tastebuds will get a treat. Even if you don't have a perfect green thumb, the quiet sanctuary of your garden can provide a necessary break from the stress of daily life with a breather of nature.

Tending to your own garden is the perfect way to introduce the fifth step of the SWITCH OFF method as we move on to examine how the foods we eat can support a life free from overthinking.

CHAPTER FIVE: C:
CONSCIOUS NOURISHMENT

We often tell ourselves that we are what we eat in an effort to maintain a balanced diet, but nutrition goes deeper than providing the body with the necessary vitamins and minerals. Diet affects sleep, mood, and cognitive function.

Nutritional deficiencies have been strongly linked to mental health conditions. A lack of B12, B9, zinc and high consumption of processed foods can increase the risk of depression (Lachance & Ramsey, 2015). This is because B vitamins and folate are essential for the happy hormones in the brain to send messages efficiently. Omega-3 fatty acids are being used to treat several conditions, including major depressive disorder, bipolar depression, and post-traumatic stress disorder (PTSD).

If you add poor sleep to an already lacking diet, the brain is in trouble. Each night, the body and brain go through a cycle of processes, and for the brain, different chemicals are released during each process. The body needs to pass three stages of non-rapid eye movement before it can fall into a state of rapid eye movement. This stage is crucial for cognition, memory, and creativity.

Disturbed sleep can interrupt these natural cycles. In the short term, this can cause difficulty concentrating, irritability, and poor memory. When it becomes a long-term problem, you may struggle with work performance and brain power, and there is a greater risk of developing dementia.

Science aside, the vicious cycle is something we have all experienced. A bad night's sleep can cause us to turn to less-healthy food options for a quick boost of energy. This is followed by an energy crash and a lack of motivation for physical activity. However, physical activity improves sleep.

The cycle has to break, and fortunately, this doesn't mean you have to go on a strict diet!

STRATEGY #16: LIFE SYNERGY FOR THE MIND

Psychonutrition is a science-based practice that combines psychology and nutrition to better understand the complexities of biochemical processes. Nutrition has traditionally focused on physical conditions, but as food is so critical for the brain's neurotransmitters and hormones, more attention is now placed on a holistic approach to mental health and diet.

Instead of treating the symptoms of mental health conditions, psycho-nutrition gets to the bottom of the problem by looking at imbalances in the body. You may want to speak to your doctor or a nutritionist to determine what imbalance or deficiency you may have. To rectify imbalances or deficiencies, you can make minor tweaks to your diet or, if needed, take supplements.

Let's begin with the role of antioxidants in our diet. The body produces free radicals, unstable molecules with an unpaired electron in their outer shells. These free radicals help the body fight infections, control blood flow in the arteries, and even help the brain stay focused. But as with everything in life, there has to be a balance.

Certain factors in our environment and lifestyle, such as pollution, smoking, drinking, radiation, and even too much sunbathing, can lead to an increase in free radicals in the body. When this occurs, free radicals can link to form chains, damage cells, and cause oxidative stress.

Oxidative stress has been linked to several health conditions, including cardiovascular disease, central nervous diseases (such as dementia), and genetic degenerative diseases (for example, Parkinson's).

Oxidative stress has consequences on the central nervous system too. On the one hand, cells in the central nervous system have limited regenerative capacity. On the other hand, neurotransmitters such as dopamine and serotonin are more susceptible to oxidation compared with cells in other parts of the body. For this reason, oxidative stress can also lead to different anxiety disorders and major depression (Das Graças Fedoce et al., 2018).

Here is where antioxidants come in! Antioxidants also have an uneven number of electrons but are less aggressive than free radicals. Antioxidants will happily donate an electron to a free radical and make it stable. For this reason, we must have enough antioxidants in our diets to ensure a balance between free radicals and antioxidants to reduce the risk of oxidative stress, not just for mental well-being but also for physical health.

A meta-analysis involving 4,049 participants over 52 studies showed that antioxidant supplements had a significant effect on both anxiety and depression (Wang et al., 2023).

One of the most common sources of antioxidants is fruits and vegetables, particularly the following:

- Cranberries/Strawberries/Blackberries/Blueberries

- Red grapes

- Cherries

- Apples

- Oranges

- Broccoli/Cabbage/Leafy greens

- Carrots/Beets/Radish

- Potatoes

- Asparagus

- Squash

- Avocados

Fresh fruit and vegetables are generally considered better but don't forget that when they are dried, they will have higher concentrations of antioxidants. Healthy snacks that can provide extra antioxidants include cereals like oatmeal and nuts, including almonds, cashews, pistachios, and walnuts. Walnuts are also a great source of healthy fats that can help improve your memory.

Antioxidants in food are measured in oxygen radical absorbance capacity (ORAC), and this is relevant because you can see just how powerful herbs and spices are for a diet rich in antioxidants.

You may have heard people talk about how amazing blueberries are for their antioxidant capacities. Wild blueberries have an ORAC value of 9,621, which sounds great. But compare this with the following ORAC values of dried herbs and spices.

- Ginger- 39,041

- Curry powder- 48,504

- Basil- 61,063

- Parsley- 73,670

- Turmeric- 127,068

- Thyme- 156,380

- Rosemary- 165,280

- Oregano- 175,295

- Ground cloves- 290,283 (Medindia, 2021)

While eating a cup full of blueberries is not the same as consuming a cup full of ground cloves, herbs, and spices are so versatile that adding them to each meal and beverage is easy. Tea and coffee are both high in antioxidants, so you can increase your intake by adding spices like cinnamon or ginger.

Turmeric is definitely a spice to consider. In addition to the high level of antioxidants, this spice can improve memory. The active ingredient, curcumin, can increase serotonin and dopamine, easing depression. It may even help the brain grow new cells. When using turmeric, always add black pepper because this significantly increases the body's ability to absorb curcumin.

There are other foods that can give your brain a boost that are only plant-based. Fatty fish have high amounts of omega-3 fatty acids that the body needs for brain and nerve cell development.

Studies have shown that omega-3 increases brain learning, memory, and blood flow (Dighriri et al., 2022). The best sources include salmon, sardines, trout, and herring. Eggs have vitamins B6 and B12, folate, and choline, micronutrients needed to make a neurotransmitter that regulates both mood and memory.

Well-being isn't just about your diet. Many medical professionals are now advocating for a holistic approach that synergizes sleep, diet, physical activity, and stress management for overall health improvements. We've already covered exercise, so let's take a deeper look at diet before combining other holistic approaches.

STRATEGY #17: MINDFUL EATING

There is a lot of talk about the Mediterranean diet and its host of health benefits, but another cultural aspect could explain their healthy lifestyles. People from these cultures tend to slow down and actually take the time to appreciate their meals, a practice now known as mindful eating.

Mindful eating focuses on the eating experience, making thoughtful choices about food, and being aware of the different sensations in the body. It gives you time to consider where your food comes from and listen to the signals your body sends to let you know when you are hungry and full, as well as how the body feels afterward. Mindful eating teaches us to slow down and savor every bite with gratitude.

Research has shown that mindful eating can reduce binge eating and emotional eating. As part of diabetes self-management education, mindful eating reduces depressive symptoms for those with type 2 diabetes (Harvard, 2020).

A popular way to practice mindful eating is with raisins; however, if you don't like raisins, you can choose another food. Whichever food it happens to be, try to imagine it's as if you're seeing it for the first time.

Hold a raisin in your hand and examine its texture, the different wrinkles, and how the color changes with the texture. Bring the raisin up to your ear. You might feel weird doing this, but does the raisin make any sound when you roll it between your fingers?

Next, smell the raisin. What does it smell like to you? Remember, this isn't what you should think it smells like! By now, you may notice that your tastebuds are more engaged. Slowly put the raisin in your mouth, but don't chew it yet. Hold it on your tongue while you concentrate on the sensations.

When you are ready, bite the raisin, focusing on the taste. As you chew, you might notice different flavors and textures. Finally, consciously decide to swallow the raisin and pay attention to how the raisin feels as it moves down your throat.

Don't worry if thoughts come to mind as you are practicing this. As with all mindful techniques, acknowledge the thoughts without judgment and return your focus to mindful eating.

STRATEGY #18: IMPROVING NUTRITION

It's not just oxidative stress that impacts stress and anxiety caused by overthinking. There is an extremely influential connection between the brain and the gut to the extent that the gut is often called "the second brain." To understand the brain-gut connection, it's necessary to go back to the central nervous system.

Two of the main parts of the central nervous system (CNS) are the sympathetic nervous system (SNS) and the parasympathetic nervous system (PNS). The SNS is responsible for our fight-or-flight mode and kicks into action when we are faced with chronic stress, fear, and anxiety. The PNS, also known as "rest and digest mode," helps the body return to a calm state once the perceived trigger has passed. It's not a case of one working while the other isn't, but more of an intricate balance between the two.

A major part of the PNS is the vagus nerve. This is the tenth cranial nerve and the longest. It gets its name from the Latin word "to wander" because it begins at the base of the spine, passes the vocal cords, and then branches into all the major organs all the way down to the gut.

Essentially, the vagus nerve is the two-way brain-gut connection along with the 100 million nerve cells that line the gastrointestinal tract as part of the enteric nervous system.

The brain contains billions of neurons, but at the same time, the gut also includes around 500 million neurons, which connect to the brain through the nervous system and neurotransmitters. It's well known that the neurotransmitters in the brain control emotions, but the trillions of microbes living in your gut also create neurotransmitters. Two of these neurotransmitters are serotonin and gamma-aminobutyric acid (GABA). GABA helps control anxiety and fear.

This intricate connection explains why some psychological and physiological symptoms and sensations are related. Nerves can be experienced as butterflies in the stomach. Anxiety might make you feel sick. At the same time, stress, anxiety, and depression can aggravate gastrointestinal conditions, even making pain worse.

In the past, digestive disorders were treated with conventional medicine, but with a better understanding of the brain-gut connection, psychology-based approaches are proving to be more effective.

Along with upping the antioxidants, overthinking can be helped by feeding the gut with essential foods that keep the trillions of microbes in your gut healthy and happy. Probiotics and prebiotics have been shown to improve gut flora and brain health.

It may seem weird, but probiotics are live bacteria and yeast. While we typically see these microorganisms as bad, probiotics are good for us, especially for the digestive system. Their role is to impact the nerves in the gut, which then helps move food through the system.

Studies have shown that 8 weeks of taking a probiotic supplement had a positive effect on major depressive disorder symptoms compared with a placebo (Akkasheh et al., 2015).

Yogurt is one of the best sources of probiotics. Milk is fermented by lactic acid and bifidobacteria. Apart from gut health, yogurt may improve bone and heart health while lowering the risk of diabetes. Make sure you choose active yogurt and those that aren't high in sugar. Kefir might seem similar to yogurt, but it's made by adding kefir grains (cultures of lactic acid and yeast) to milk.

Sauerkraut is a cabbage that has been shredded and fermented by lactic acid bacteria. It actually tastes much nicer than it sounds. Pickles or gherkins are cucumbers left to ferment, thanks to the lactic acid bacteria they contain. Pickles that have been left in vinegar don't have probiotic effects.

Several probiotic foods come from the use of soy products. Tempeh is a fermented soybean product that is often used as a meat substitute because, during fermentation, B12 is produced. A Japanese treat, miso is a seasoning made by fermenting soybeans with a fungus called koji and salt. Again, it tastes nicer than it sounds.

Prebiotics act as food for the microorganisms in your gut. When different types of prebiotics are broken down, they create different short-chain fatty acids that do various jobs in the body, such as reducing inflammation and boosting immunity. Much research is still needed on the different types of prebiotics. Still, one study showed how galactooligosaccharides (GOS) reduced the amount of cortisol in the body (Schmidt et al., 2014).

GOS prebiotics are plant sugars linked in chains and can be found in legumes, beans, some root vegetables, cashew and pistachios nuts, and soy and oat milk. To make sure you are getting a wide range of prebiotics, try including more or the following foods:

- Almonds

- Bananas

- Whole grains

- Flax

- Cabbage

- Peas

- Raw garlic

- Raw onion

- Oats

- Honey

- Agave

Prebiotics are added to cereals, breads, and snack foods. It will help if you look out for GOS, FOS (fructooligosaccharides), and TOS (transgalactooligosaccharides) on food labels. Other added prebiotics can include acacia gum, inulin, polydextrose, psyllium, and wheat dextrin.

Let's finish this strategy with just a few brain-boosting recipes. I haven't listed the exact ingredients because I think it's best that people adjust to suit their own tastebuds.

Turmeric Oats

Add oats, soy milk, bananas, a good sprinkle of ground cinnamon, and a 4-inch piece of freshly grated turmeric to a blender. If you can't find fresh turmeric, use 2 teaspoons of ground powder. Next, add 1 ½ cups of soy milk and ½ cups of water and blend well. You can take some chopped nuts and sprinkle them on top for an extra boost.

Aromatic Lamb

Finely chop the onion and add to a frying pan with a bit of oil. Once the onions are soft, add lamb cut into cubes and cook for around 10 minutes. Aromatic spices to add include cumin seeds, garlic, ginger, cayenne pepper, cloves, and cinnamon. Add a tin of chopped tomatoes and 1 cup of water. Place a lid on the pan and allow it to simmer for an hour, adding more water if necessary.

Lentil and Beet Salad

Cook the lentils according to the packet instructions and leave them to cool. Slice the cooked beetroot (not in vinegar) and add it to the lentils. In a bowl, make a dressing out of wholegrain mustard and extra virgin oil. Pour it over the lentils and mix well.

A healthy brain helps you sleep better, but better sleep is also essential for a healthy brain. As we move on to the next strategy, it's time to discover how to realistically improve sleep.

STRATEGY #19: SLEEP OPTIMIZATION & TECHNIQUES FOR BETTER SLEEP

There are two processes that control sleep. One is your sleep drive, and the other is the circadian rhythm. Sleep drive is the body's need for sleep as the day progresses, much like hunger. However, you have less control over your sleep drive as you do hunger. Once your body reaches a certain point of exhaustion, you need to sleep!

Interestingly, when you are at the limit of exhaustion, you can have microsleeps, where you can sleep with your eyes open for just a second or two. It's recommended not to nap for more than 30 minutes because longer naps can disrupt the body's sleep drive.

The circadian rhythm is the body's biological clock, a part of the brain that responds to light. At night, the circadian rhythm produces more melatonin (the sleep hormone), but once light is detected, it stops producing this hormone.

Once asleep, the sleep cycle has four stages, split into non-rapid eye movement (NREM) and rapid eye movement (REM). The first stage lasts for a few minutes, the moment you drift off to sleep. Stage 2 is light sleep, which can last from 10 minutes to an hour when the brain and body gradually become less active. These two stages of NREM are the easiest to wake up from.

The third stage of NREM lasts 20 to 40 minutes, and this is the deep sleep stage. At this time, the brain's activity is at its slowest. The fourth is the only stage of REM, and crazy things happen in these 10 to 60 minutes. Brain activity picks up, resulting in your most vivid dreams. Arms and legs are temporarily paralyzed. This is to prevent the body from acting out the dreams!

Typically, these stages are repeated four or five times per night. As the night progresses, we spend more time in REM. During this stage, the central nervous system is activated, preparing us to wake up. Because of this, it's easy to wake up at this stage. It's important to note that each stage is important in the sleep cycle, but it's the third stage that allows for physical and mental restoration.

Overthinking can have two dramatic impacts on the sleep cycle. In the first place, it's more than likely that overthinking interferes with sleep drive.

You are probably familiar with the dreaded feeling of being completely drained, but your mind refuses to quiet down enough for you to fall asleep. Overthinking causes stress and anxiety to activate the sympathetic nervous system, so the parasympathetic nervous system can't let the body rest and digest!

Secondly, overthinking can make it impossible to fall asleep again if you wake up in the middle of the night. Ironically, you may even find yourself overthinking about the lack of sleep and how difficult the next day will be.

According to the Sleep Foundation, it should take no more than 20 minutes to fall asleep when you go to bed (Rausch-Phung & Rehman, 2023), and if you wake up during the night, you should be able to fall asleep again within 15 to 30 minutes. No pun intended...but that sounds like a dream!

So we are back to one of those vicious cycles. A lack of sleep feeds anxiety, and anxiety can negatively impact sleep! When the body and mind don't get enough sleep, the levels of cortisol in the body increase. Insomnia is associated with generalized anxiety disorder, depression, PTSD, and panic disorder.

How much sleep a person needs will vary. Most adults need between 7 and 9 hours of sleep, but some need as few as 6 or as many as 10. Before calculating the hours of sleep you need, it's worth remembering that sleep debt is a real thing.

If you lose a certain number of hours of sleep over a few nights, you must make up for those lost hours at some point. For this reason, it's worth tracking your sleep patterns over several days, if not weeks. You can monitor your sleep using a smartwatch or any sleep-tracking app or device.

Based on allowing for 15 minutes to fall asleep and 5 sleep cycles of 90 minutes each, a person waking up at 6 a.m. would need to go to bed at 10:15 p.m., waking up at 6:15 a.m. means going to bed at 10.30 p.m., and so on.

For those who need around 9 hours of sleep, this would mean 6 cycles of 15 minutes. Waking up at 6 a.m. means a bedtime of 8:45 p.m., and 6:15 a.m. would mean going to bed at 9 p.m., etc.

This isn't your first rodeo, so it would be insulting to tell you to avoid caffeine and have a good bedtime routine. Let's focus on the less obvious.

The Ideal Sleep Environment

What one person considers ideal will differ from the next, but a good temperature is between 60 and 68 degrees

Fahrenheit. There are several nice extras that can create a relaxed environment. You might want to experiment with essential oils, a quiet fan, or other types of white noise.

If your mattress is over 10 years old, you might want to consider a new one and ensure you use a suitable quilt material for the season. Some people have had success with weighted blankets to help with anxiety.

Clear Your Mind Before Going to Bed

We have looked at several ways to help "empty" the brain, and now is the time to put these techniques into action. A healthy bedtime routine can begin with scheduling time for worry. Take 5 to 10 minutes to purposely worry, but make sure you pay attention to the take and don't allow yourself to worry for longer.

Also, try to leave at least an hour between the scheduled worry time and bedtime. A brain dump (writing down your thoughts) is highly beneficial, and on a more practical note, creating a to-do list for the following day will prevent you from going to bed worrying about forgetting something.

Support Your Circadian Rhythm

A dark room helps the circadian rhythm and doesn't provide the body with the wrong cues to wake up, but there is a particular light that stops the production of melatonin. Blue light from our devices also prevents the production of melatonin. It might be a hard habit to ditch, but keeping phones and tablets beside the bed is unhealthy. If we are honest with ourselves, scrolling through social media can often fuel overthinking, so there are two good reasons to move our devices away.

Progressive Muscle Relaxation

Research has shown that progressive muscle relaxation can improve sleep quality and induce slow-wave-rich sleep (Simon et al., 2022). Slow-wave rich sleep is like the VIP section of your sleep party. During this stage, your brain waves slow down, which helps your body repair muscles, release growth hormones, and organize memories. If you don't get enough of this type of sleep, you may wake up feeling groggy and struggle to think clearly.

It's best to do this technique while in bed so it's easy to drift off. Beginning with your toes, tense all the muscles and hold them for a few seconds before releasing the tension. Follow this by tensing all the muscles in your feet and holding them before releasing the tension. Repeat the same with all muscle pairs as you make your way up the body, finishing with the facial muscles.

Guided Meditation for Sleep

Here are a few videos that can guide you to fall into a deeper sleep faster.

SCAN ME

Guided Sleep Meditation

Know When to Be in Bed and When Not to

Although we have covered the ideal time to go to bed to ensure you get enough sleep, you also can't force the sleep drive. Going to bed if you aren't tired is like giving your brain permission, even encouragement to overthink.

If you wake up in the middle of the night and it's been more than 30 minutes, you should get up so that the bed doesn't become a place of stress. If you do have to get up, choose relaxing activities, such as meditation, relaxation yoga, and affirmations. It's ideal to choose activities that do not reward the brain, such as watching your favorite series.

Consulting Your Doctor

If you have taken all the necessary steps, including limiting caffeine, alcohol, and smoking, and managing overthinking, but chronic sleep issues are still a problem, it is worth talking to your doctor. Certain medications can impact sleep, such as some asthma treatments, antidepressants, beta-blockers, and steroid medications. It's also better to be safe than sorry and rule out any medical conditions that could affect your ability to sleep.

10-Minute Meditation For Sleep

Mindfulness Sleep Meditation

The final strategy in this chapter will not only help with sleep but also manage those challenging moments during the day when the brain feels the need to go into overdrive.

STRATEGY #20: STRESS MANAGEMENT

For one final time, we are going to go back to the nervous system to discover how some simple techniques can manage stress, whether you are preparing for an important meeting or getting ready for bed!

The fight-or-flight response may seem like your worst nightmare, but from our evolutionary standpoint, it has kept previous generations safe and alive. In today's world, many of our stressors are perceived threats, but the brain doesn't distinguish the difference.

Overthinking about a future event can cause the body to react in the same way it would when you walk down a dark alley and hear footsteps behind you.

Your heart rate increases, breathing becomes shallow, and a rush of adrenaline is released. Peripheral vision is heightened, hearing becomes more acute, and muscles tense. This hyperactive fight-or-flight response leads to a constant state of anxiety, making it easier to overreact to perceived threats. It can also lead to increased blood pressure, clogged arteries, and a greater risk of heart disease and heart attacks.

What many don't realize is that these effects on the body don't just stop when the stressor is no longer present. In fact, the parasympathetic nervous system can take anywhere from 20 to 60 minutes to return the body to its calm state (Cherry, 2022). To mitigate the effects of stress on the body, we can turn to our longest cranial nerve!

The vagus nerve makes up around 75 percent of the nerve tissues in the parasympathetic nervous system. Stimulating it helps the body return to rest and digest quicker.

Vagus Nerve Stimulation

Splashing cold water on your face sounds like an old myth, but it does work! Because the vagus nerve passes the vocal cords, you may find that singing, humming, and gargling also help to manage stress.

Deep Breathing

1. Find yourself a comfortable position, either sitting or lying down
2. Slowly breathe in through your nose until your lungs and chest feel full
3. Hold your breath for a few seconds
4. Slowly exhale through your nose
5. Place one hand on your chest and the other on your belly
6. Repeat your deep breath, noticing how your hands move up and down as you breathe
7. Continue for 5 or 6 more deep breaths

Guided Imagery

Choose a quiet place, get comfortable, close your eyes, and begin deep breathing. The success of guided imagery comes down to the image you choose to picture. It has to be an environment that is incredibly peaceful and meaningful to you. It could be a log cabin in the woods, a crystal clear beach, or sitting next to the fireplace in your family home.

Picture yourself fully in that place and use all your senses to engage in the environment. The more detail you can imagine about the area and your surroundings, the more effective this technique is. Once you have relaxed for as long as you can, bring your mind back to the present.

Stress management is very personal, and what works for one may not always be a solution for the next. Anything from exercise to aromatherapy and hugs to gratitude journaling can help manage stress.

For a personalized stress management plan, you need to be aware of the stress cycle, what fuels the stress, and what provides relief. When we experience stress and discomfort, we react with a coping strategy. This strategy will either be negative or positive.

If your coping strategy is negative, you will end up feeling more discomfort. However, a positive coping strategy is like lifting some of the weight off your shoulders.

Because positive coping strategies are unique to each individual, a good habit is to start completing a stress management tracker to begin your stress management plan. Create a list of stress management techniques that you feel would benefit you personally.

Here are some potential ideas:

• Listen to music

• Dance

• Prepare a healthy meal

• 4-8-7 breathing

• Guided meditation

• Laughing

• Spending time in nature

• Squeezing a stress ball

• Engaging your senses

- Positive affirmations

- Brain dump

- Talking to someone

Make a note of the level of your initial level of stress on a scale of one to ten. After practicing one of the stress management techniques, make another note of your stress level. By doing this, you will be able to pinpoint activities that provide the greatest stress relief.

Unfortunately, one potential source of stress comes from the people in our lives, even those we love the most. By the end of the next chapter, you can set fair and healthy limits that will give you mental space and energy while reducing situations that can lead to overthinking.

CHAPTER SIX: H: HEALTHY LIMITS

How often has someone asked you to do something you didn't want, causing you to spend hours overthinking it? Or what about the people who continuously do things that you don't like? The result isn't just rumination, frustration, and self-criticism.

When you don't have personal limits, life can quickly become unbalanced. You may feel like you are walking on eggshells and that others are draining any energy to manage to accumulate. Instead of doing things you enjoy, you are stuck doing things that negatively impact your mental health and physical health. For example, if you need a night in for self-care and relaxation but can't say no to a friend, you are suffering.

Many people don't set limits because they fear disapproval and rejection. Saying no to someone could make them upset, angry, or even ignore you, which goes against what all humans crave: love and acceptance.

In reality, these limits are crucial for respect as well as self-respect. You have the right to put your own needs and desires first. It's not selfish to prioritize your own well-being so that you can be at your best. Boundaries are the first step!

STRATEGY #21: BOUNDARY-SETTING

Boundaries let other people know your limits and are necessary for protecting your physical and emotional space while giving you a sense of control over your life. There are six types of boundaries:

- **Emotional boundaries:** These boundaries protect your feelings. They can help you decide what information you are comfortable sharing and the topics you don't want to discuss. Emotional boundaries allow you to help others in distress but not take responsibility for how they feel.

- **Physical boundaries:** It's important for others to know your comfort levels with personal space and physical contact and be aware of what is appropriate for different relationships and situations.

- **Sexual boundaries:** Regardless of gender, age, or culture, everyone has the right to express their sexual boundaries, including touching, kissing, and when to say no to sex. Not adhering to sexual boundaries can be a form of sexual assault.

- **Time boundaries:** You also have the right to decide how to spend your time so that you can create a healthy work-life balance. Time boundaries can include your free time, vacations, and not putting up with people who are constantly late.

• **Material boundaries: T**his refers to your personal property, what you are comfortable letting other people use or borrow, and clearly defining the terms involved. Material boundaries include your personal finances.

• **Intellectual boundaries:** Intellectual boundaries are a common source of conflict that covers religious, spiritual, and political views as well as respect for thoughts and ideas. Everybody has the right to their own opinions, and they should be respected, even if others don't agree.

Before understanding what your own limits are, it's necessary to consider your level of self-differentiation. Self-differentiation is the ability to see yourself as an individual from others. A good example is how we often grow up with the same views and opinions as long-term friends, family members, and parents.

For example, do you support a particular political party because you agree with their policies or because your parents support them? Self-differentiation is about living according to your true self. Consider these journal prompts:

1. In what ways are you not living in the way you want to?
2. What do you need or want more of in your life?
3. What is stopping you from growing?
4. What would you be doing if you could do anything in a year?
5. Who in your life holds you back from realizing your dreams?

6. List 5 things you wish others knew about you but don't feel confident to say.
7. What obstacles are in the way of your happiness?
8. What are some things others do that cause you to overthink?

The answers to these questions will help you determine your boundaries. As well as self-differentiation, you should create an internal social comfort scale. Use a scale from 1 to 4, with 4 being comfortable and 1 being uncomfortable.

Imagine dating someone new. Your level 4 might be meeting for coffee, level 3 dinner, level 2 meeting friends, and level 1 meeting family. It doesn't mean that you will never be ready to meet friends and family; it just means that you are more aware of your current levels of comfort so that you can communicate this with others.

Begin by creating a list of the boundaries you want to set. These boundaries should be in order of priority, but also consider that it's easier to start with smaller boundaries and with those you feel more confident about. Ensure your boundaries are in line with your values, as this will make it easier to communicate without feeling guilty.

Be clear about the boundary. When others are uncertain about your limits, it can be difficult for someone to respect them. At the same time, there is no need to overcomplicate things or say more than you need to. You shouldn't feel the need to justify your boundaries. It helps to practice what you want to say beforehand.

Communicating the boundary can be the most daunting. Stick to using "I" statements that keep the focus on your emotions rather than the actions of others. For example, "I feel frustrated when you insist on making sexist jokes."

Don't apologize for setting your boundaries because this implies that you are doing something wrong by prioritizing your needs. Because your boundaries are in place to protect your well-being rather than control others, there is no need for you to feel bad for having them. Reminding yourself of this will help you communicate your boundaries with confidence.

This is often enough, but there will be people who don't respect your boundaries, and consequences must be enforced. For boundaries to be effective, you have to follow through on the consequences!

Spend more time with those who respect your boundaries, as this will remind you of what healthy boundaries look like and that having them is not a selfish act!

STRATEGY #22: SAYING NO

In today's society, it seems that saying no is often viewed as a bad thing and considered audacious! Like boundary setting, saying no is a sign of assertiveness, which isn't the same as being rude. Being assertive means taking into account other people's thoughts and feelings into consideration while also standing up for one's personal points of view or objectives.

It's a skill that requires clear, firm communication and has two significant benefits. First, being able to say no reduces anxious thoughts. How many times have you found yourself saying yes to something and then spending the rest of the day dreading what was to come? Second, assertiveness allows you to experience a full spectrum of emotions without reacting aggressively or passively.

The traits of an assertive person include:

- Being honest about their thoughts and feelings

- Actively listening to consider different perspectives

- Remaining in control of feelings, even when others don't

- Admit when they have made mistakes

Though it sounds straightforward, before asserting your "no," you have to learn when to say yes and when to say no. To do this, it's worth looking back at some past situations. Ask yourself, "When did I say yes when I should have said no?" This could be anything from an hour of overtime to a marriage proposal.

Next, consider the impact the "yes" had on your life. Again, this impact could be relatively small to life-changing. It could have meant not being home to read your children their bedtime story to 10 years in a loveless marriage before a painful divorce.

Take some extra time to reflect on why you may have felt you couldn't say no in a particular situation. This may be due to various reasons, such as the need to fit in or feel loved, concerns about potential repercussions, or a strong sense of obligation to do something.

If you delve a little deeper, you may find that your difficulty in saying no comes from learned behaviors from your childhood in order for you to feel safe and loved.

What can be equally as damaging is not saying yes when you should. There will be circumstances in life where you don't feel confident saying yes. Imagine being offered a promotion and not saying yes because of a fear of imposter syndrome. A wise person once said that you should always say yes to the most important person in your life, which is you!

To decide whether you should say yes or no, consider if the request fits in with your short-term or long-term goals and evaluate the pros and cons of both the yes and the no. It goes without saying that you should never feel obliged to give an answer straight away, and if you need time to think about a response, take it, even if it's just 5 minutes.

Be careful of those fears and cognitive distortions taking over. You may feel the urge to succumb to societal pressures or make a decision based on the need to be liked rather than respected. Even though fear might be overwhelming, always remember that you have the power to control your emotions.

There are two ways to assertively say no. The first is to practice what you want to say. This could be something like, "I respect your opinion, but I don't agree because…" or "Thank you for the invitation, but I'm afraid I have other things to do."

Knowing exactly what you want to say beforehand reduces the risk of talking too much or overexplaining your "no." When this happens, others may see this as an opportunity to persuade or push.

This leads to the second technique, simply to say no as a single word and a complete sentence on its own. Body language and tone of voice are crucial in assertiveness, but more so if you are going just to say no.

Picture the difference between someone with an abrupt tone, chest puffed out, and one eyebrow raised. Their "no" comes across as aggressive. If it's a timid "no" with hunched shoulders and no eye contact, it may not be taken seriously.

Whether you are practicing a more extended response or using just one word, be sure to stand straight, hold steady eye contact, and have a warm facial expression. Speak loud enough for the person to hear your steady voice but without over-projecting your voice and inadvertently attracting attention.

If you like the idea of just saying no but need a little practice building up to this, here are some short phrases to say no without the actual word:

- I wish I could

- I'm afraid I can't

- I have another commitment

- Ask me in a week/month

- Sadly, I have something else going on

- That's not going to work for me

- Not this time

- If only there were two of me

- I'm not the right person for that

- Thanks for thinking of me, but it's not possible

Fortunately, these phrases will also work wonders when it comes to the next strategy and overcoming the need to please others constantly.

STRATEGY #23: NO TO PEOPLE PLEASING

Not being able to say no is a vital sign of people pleasing, especially when making others happy comes at a cost to your own well-being. Helping others makes you feel good, but it's important to recognize this as temporary happiness.

Eventually, prioritizing others' needs leads to less time for your own interests. There is no balance, and you will find yourself neglecting your physical and emotional needs. When people take advantage of your kindness, you may also end up feeling resentment and responding with passive aggression.

Poor self-esteem and a lack of self-worth can result from people pleasing, but they can also be a cause. Like not being able to say no, people pleasing creates immense stress and anxiety due to the fear of what others think about you and the need for approval.

Other signs of people pleasing include frequently saying sorry or feeling guilty about things that aren't your fault. This might be linked to perfectionism and the need to ensure everything is right for others. You may also notice a fear of rejection and going out of your way to avoid it.

The first steps to stop people pleasing are to ensure your boundaries are in place and that you have the confidence to assertively say no. If you feel that these steps aren't as effective as you had hoped, it's time to take a moment to be alone and reconsider your boundaries, ensuring they align with your values, needs, and wishes, and then reevaluate the consequences you have in place.

Imagine your friend has a habit of showing up late, and you have explained how this makes you feel, but he continues disrespecting your boundaries. You need to reinforce the boundary with a consequence, but this will only have the desired effect if you follow through with it. If you tell your friend you won't wait for him but still stay, it shows your boundaries are weak.

The question to ask yourself is whether you have enough self-esteem and self-worth to believe you deserve boundaries. Self-worth is harder to improve, mainly because of how we define it.

Subconsciously or not, we compare ourselves to others, and this can lead to thinking of our self-worth as a reflection of our job title, paycheck, or what happens on our social media. While these things may have a role in life, they aren't as important as compassion, empathy, and respect— qualities that people pleasers have an abundance of.

If your negative inner critic is eating away at your self-worth, go back to strategy #11 to review the steps of cognitive reconstruction in order to reframe unhelpful thoughts. Try turning some of that outer kindness you constantly show others onto yourself!

Journal Prompts for Self-Worth

- In what moments do you tend to compare yourself to others?

- When are you most critical about yourself? Considering negativity bias and other cognitive distortions, is this fair?

- Reflect on times when you feel insecure and think about what triggers this.

- What situations cause you to be someone you aren't so that you feel accepted?

- In which situations do you think your self-worth increases?

When answering these questions, you might feel that you have certain weaknesses, which is why your self-worth is so low. There is no such thing as weaknesses; there are only areas for improvement.

The internet has made it possible to improve almost any skill through online courses, forums, or even TED Talks. Be proactive about your areas of improvement so that you can see just how capable you are.

The first skill to boost self-worth is the ability to say no to something you don't want to do. You will build yourself up and probably feel nervous, even scared, but the moment you kindly yet firmly say no is the moment you can truly start seeing yourself in a different light.

For both self-worth and self-esteem, remember the FAST skill, an acronym used in dialectical behavioral therapy, that improves communication while maintaining your values and self-respect.

- **F**: Be **Fair.** Be fair to others and the situation, but also be fair to yourself. Keep to the facts so that your own needs and values aren't overlooked by the opinions of others.

- **A**: Don't over **Apologize.** Apologize for the mistakes you make, if you accidentally upset someone, or if you are wrong. Don't apologize for your feelings or having a different opinion.

- **S**: **Stick** to your values. Your values, morals, needs, and wants aren't up for debate, and compromising them may provide a quick fix, but in the long run, you will get hurt.

- **T**: Be **Truthful.** Combine your newly developed assertiveness with some courage, and always be honest. It's just as important to be honest with yourself as with others!

On the positive side, the next time someone praises you or pays you a compliment, accept it. We often tend to brush off these positive comments or disregard them.

If you doubt your self-worth, remember this: if your partner didn't love you, they wouldn't be with you; if your friends didn't value you, they wouldn't be around; and if your boss didn't appreciate you, you wouldn't be paid!

One way to help overcome an inaccurate idea of self-worth is to set some additional boundaries with technology and how you use it.

STRATEGY #24: DIGITAL DISCIPLINE

Before looking at the downsides, there is no doubt that technology can have an immensely positive impact on our lives, especially regarding work and education. How we use technology can shape our brains the same way our thoughts do. Using digital devices for learning, research, and creativity can strengthen our neural connections, making us smarter.

Scrolling for the sake of scrolling can weaken crucial synapses, leading to reduced attention and weaker memory. Research has shown that not only can heavy digital use impact attention, but it can also lead to less cognitive control. The mind struggles to focus on what is important (Open Colleges, 2016).

Unfortunately, all of this can also impact relationships and interactions. A lack of attention and being easily distracted can lower levels of empathy, as conversations and connections don't have the same depth.

At the same time, there is a risk of cognitive overload regardless of what you are using technology for. Working memory, the part of the brain that temporarily holds information for the task at hand, can only hold so much. The bombardment of information online can make it more difficult to concentrate, and less gets done!

In a world where technology is becoming more and more dominant, it's crucial to practice digital discipline. However, this is often one area of boundary setting that is forgotten. Consider the following points before you jump online:

• What is the purpose of being online? This might be simple if you need to work and put food on the table; however, you could still ask yourself if it is essential at that very moment! If you are using social media, is the purpose to connect with someone close to you? Do you need all 500+ "friends" knowing the ins and outs of your life?

• Set yourself a time boundary! It's easy to say "5 minutes", and an hour later, you are still scrolling. If it's work-related, using the Pomodoro technique of 25 minutes online followed by a 5-minute break can increase productivity. If it's for social use, set an alarm and be strict with yourself.

• Take advantage of functions on your phone and other apps, such as Do Not Disturb, and switch off notifications that may distract you. Change the settings on app controls so that you can only use them for a certain amount of time.

• Structure your day so that online activities are separated from offline activities to avoid information overload and screen fatigue.

• Don't eat while on devices. Use this time for a proper break from technology.

• Don't take devices to bed. The blue light emitted by screens can impact melatonin production!

Finally, get into the habit of treating your use of technology like your favorite indulgence. The occasional cream cake every now and then won't harm you too much, and digital devices are the same—all in moderation! That being said, when the addiction gets too much, it's time for a detox!

STRATEGY #25: DIGITAL DETOX

As the name suggests, a digital detox is a determined amount of time away from technology. Research has shown that a social media detox can improve sleep and mood and reduce anxiety both during the detox and immediately after (El-Khoury et al., 2020).

Another study suggested that limiting the amount of time you spend on social media to 30 minutes a day can have surprisingly positive effects and not just on well-being. Participants noticed a decrease in loneliness and symptoms of depression (Hunt ct al., 2018), which links to improved connections and empathy.

To gain a better understanding of whether you would benefit from a digital detox, answer the following questions truthfully, and remember that nobody is judging you!

• Do you feel stressed or anxious when you can't find your phone?

• Do you feel the need to check your phone every few minutes?

• Does social media make you feel angry or depressed?

• Are you concerned about likes, comments, and shares?

• Do you worry about missing out if you don't check your devices?

• Do your devices affect your sleep?

• Are you able to concentrate on one thing without the need to check your phone?

If setting boundaries with technology hasn't resolved your technostress, you can try a detox method that suits you, and there are many ways to do this.

The first is a digital fast, which means you give up all devices for some time, even up to a week. Your digital detox could be recurring, perhaps for one specific day per week. You can choose to detox from certain apps, sites, games, or even devices, only using your laptop for work and keeping your phone out of sight. Or you could go for a complete social media detox.

Steps to Take Before a Digital Detox

1. Turn off your push notifications to reduce distractions
2. Set your phone to black and white to reduce the appeal
3. Start small by putting phones away during meals
4. Ban technology from the bedroom and create other technology no-zones in your home
5. Clean up social media accounts so that your contacts are only those who bring you joy
6. Use apps like Screen Time or Digital Wellbeing to limit the time you can spend on apps
7. Plan a time for no technology in advance
8. Plan a time for offline activities to prevent boredom

Choosing a method that doesn't lead to more significant stress is crucial! For example, diving straight into a 24-hour detox may lead to more overthinking and anxiety. If this is the case, it's best to start small and build up the time. You could go for a walk for 30 minutes without using your phone or read 10 pages of your book.

The goal is to divide your overall activity into manageable steps without multitasking or checking your phone often. Make sure you have activities and things to do that provide distractions for when you are detoxing.

For some, giving up devices for extended periods of time, regardless of how enthusiastic you might be, isn't practical because of work commitments. If this is the case, you can still practice digital detoxing in the evenings, on weekends, or when your schedule allows. Going digital-free for one hour each evening is an excellent example to set for the family!

Finally, the success of your digital detox can be greatly improved when you let others know you are doing it, especially if it's for short, regular periods of time. We often pick up our phones and send a message that is less than urgent. When others know you are detoxing, they can save forwarding that hilarious meme for later. You never know, you may even encourage them to start their own digital detox!

Setting and enforcing your limits can have profound psychological consequences. It can feel like a weight lifted off your shoulders and your mind!

It's worth using your journal to track your progress, particularly the immense freedom and sense of control you can now enjoy. Health limits are choices you make. In the next chapter, we will discover three more strategies that can positively influence our choices in life.

CHAPTER SEVEN: O: OPTIMAL CHOICES

Our choices are essentially influenced by our thoughts, experiences, beliefs, and emotions. When making a decision, the brain goes back to the incredible power of neuroplasticity.

Every new experience we have creates a new connection between neurons in the brain. Some connections can become stronger as they are repeated, others weaken and eventually are eliminated, known as synaptic pruning.

How does this relate to choices? It means that the choices you made in the past have no reflection on the choices you make today. In the past, you may have made a wrong choice (more likely several), but with the brain's plasticity, you can eliminate those neural pathways and create new ones that serve for better decisions.

For this to happen, we have to cut the brain some slack! With around 86 billion neurons, each capable of creating approximately 250 connections, there is a possibility of

21,500 billion connections. That's more connections than there are stars in the Milky Way!

To get better at making the right choices, it's necessary to begin by recognizing decision fatigue and preventing it.

STRATEGY #26: MASTERING DECISIONS

It's easy to spot the signs of exhaustion, but have you ever wondered how much of it comes down to decision fatigue?

Decision fatigue is a phenomenon where people get physically, mentally, and emotionally exhausted by the decisions they have to make throughout the day. This can occur when you have to make too many decisions, your decisions can affect other people, or you are going through a difficult time in your life. It may also arise when perfectionism and procrastination lead to overthinking about decisions.

There is no way to avoid decision-making. Delaying the inevitable will only add to stress levels. To prevent decision fatigue, it's necessary to improve decision-making skills. You can begin with the WRAP method:

Step 1: Widen your options

This may sound counterproductive, but it's often the case that we come up with only solutions A or solution B, and neither of these is ideal. Thinking outside the box and looking for more creative solutions can lead to a more effective solution. Avoid going to the other extreme of having too many options; ideally, three or four ideas are best.

Step 2: Reality check

This step ensures you don't make ill-informed decisions by testing potential assumptions. Look for the facts in each of your solutions. Play out the scenarios of each, paying close attention to any biases that may get in the way.

Step 3: Attain distance

Emotions can hinder the decision-making process, and although emotions shouldn't necessarily be excluded, they should be kept in perspective.

Imagine what other people would do in your situation. Rather than focusing on your emotions, consider whether your final decision aligns with your values. And instead of relying on your present emotions, think about how your decision will make you feel at various stages in the future.

Step 4: Prepare to be wrong

In any one day, you can make over 35,000 decisions. If you were to make 35,000 math calculations, you would expect some to be wrong. It's no different with decision-making.

Mistakes provide opportunities for learning and growth. If a decision doesn't go your way, use your energy more efficiently and look at what you could have done for an alternative outcome instead of beating yourself up!

You can reduce the number of less significant decisions in two simple ways. The first is to automate some of your routine decisions. For instance, if you struggle to decide what to wear in the morning, create a section in your wardrobe that is only for work clothes.

If you spend a lot of time deciding what to cook, make a meal plan at the beginning of the week. Similarly, if you ask yourself daily whether or not you should go to the gym, stop asking the question and tell yourself that you are going.

Secondly, it's time to delegate some of these smaller decisions to other people. Don't feel like you always have to be the person to come up with a plan. When a friend asks you where to meet, have them suggest the place. In a partnership, there is always talk of dividing household chores, but the same should apply to decision-making, and allowing children to make decisions teaches them responsibility.

Cognitive Bias in Decision Making

Prospect theory is an economic concept in which a person places more value on a perceived gain than on a perceived loss. Imagine being offered $10 to keep and $20 but having to give $10 back. Prospect theory suggests we would take the $10 because giving back half of the larger amount may create emotional stress, even though the financial gain is the same.

At the same time, the prospect theory highlights how humans prefer certainty to probability. If we were given $10 and possibly won $20, we would choose the safer, more guaranteed option.

This theory sounds like it is a good thing and that it would actually help with smart decision-making, but in fact, it is a type of bias. By discounting or ignoring outcomes with a low probability, you are making decisions without all of the information. In the real world, you run the risk of taking the safest option but missing out on potential opportunities.

Secondly, be aware of the ambiguity effect. This bias is a tendency to make decisions based on a lack of information. When information is missing or unavailable, people will also tend to choose the safest option or the one they perceive to have the most gain.

A classic example of the ambiguity effect is following the 'rule of thumb' in order to reach a conclusion quickly. Again, the risk is that the conclusion or decision you get will be inaccurate or misinformed.

Those decisions that require little thought, such as meal planning and what to wear, shouldn't involve overthinking. You can afford to set a time limit and even not have all the information. To avoid the prospect theory and ambiguity effect biases, the bigger decisions in life shouldn't be rushed. Take your time to gather as much information as you can and ask people for their opinions if you are unaware of your bias.

What Are Your Priorities?

When asked to think of your priorities, it's common to think only inside the box. If you are a parent, your priority will be your children. When you wake up in the morning, your priorities may be focused on work. These tend to ignore what actually matters to your personal, bigger picture.

Let's take a look at how to review your priorities so you know where to focus your decision-making efforts.

- **Step 1:** Assess your values to know what is important to you, what you believe in, and what you stand for.

- **Step 2:** Review your strengths and areas for improvement. What will you be able to achieve once you start turning these areas into strengths?

- **Step 3:** Consider why you do what you do for a living. Does your job align with your personal values?

- **Step 4:** Separate urgent from important. Urgent tasks often come from the expectations of others, and you have a habit of taking over what's important to you.

- **Step 5:** Think before you make any commitment. Remember how people pleasing drains you or your own time for your priorities.

- **Step 6:** Write a "not-to-do list" so you have a visual reminder of the things that you need to say no to.

- **Step 7:** Set priorities based on month or season rather than trying to do too much at once. For example, if your priority is to read more, set this for winter when it's cozy to curl up on the sofa while it's raining outside.

- **Step 8:** Expect the unexpected. Allow for "nothing time" in your day in case something comes up that affects your planned schedule.

- **Step 9:** Regularly check in with your values, goals, and priorities since they will change over time.

Use the chart below to brainstorm some of your priorities. Carve out time once a month to spend even just 10 minutes to think about the 3 Cs:

- **Continue:** Consider the things that are going well and you want to keep doing

- **Come along:** Reflect on the aspects of your life that need improvement

- **Change:** Think about things that aren't working for you or aren't in line with your values

Continue	Come Along	Change

STRATEGY #27: EMBRACING CHANGE & UNCERTAINTY

In recent years, it's hard to find a human on the planet who hasn't had to face some extreme and sudden changes, and geopolitics suggests there is more uncertainty on the way.

The brain is wired to resist change. The amygdala, the part of the brain responsible for the fight-or-flight response, sees change as a form of threat and reacts the same way as it would with a genuine threat.

This can lead to ambiguity aversion, a bias that encourages us to always take the safer over a potentially easy and better one because at least we know what to expect. Choosing the safest option may seem wise in certain situations, but unless it's a life-threatening situation, you may find yourself in more mental stress than before.

Imagine you are faced with a career change. The first option means you won't have to commute as far. The other option requires irregular hours and the need to improve your skills but a higher income and opportunities for advancement. Taking the safest option means the risk of missing out on so much.

At the same time, there will be times of change that can't be avoided, and there will be no safe or easy option. Without the ability to adapt and change, you will be stuck in a cycle of discomfort.

Emotional Desensitization

The discomfort can be made worse and even prolonged by resisting change and uncertainty. Before attempting to accept change, it's essential to gradually desensitize yourself from the pain caused by uncertainty.

Emotional pain only lasts a few minutes. This sounds impossible, considering how long it lasts, but if you look at it from a different perspective, it's how you hold on to the emotional pain that makes it last so much longer. Take a negative comment you receive. It can feel like a huge stab in the heart at the time, but the dull ache continues as you dwell on that comment.

Emotional desensitization is similar to gradual exposure. It's one thing to appreciate that change is good for us, but it's another to actively go out and start making these changes without emotional suffering.

To overcome this, begin with small changes that aren't necessarily crucial. If you are used to driving a certain way to work, change your route. Sit with this discomfort as you step out of your comfort zone until changing your route no longer unnerves you. You can then move on to a slightly larger change and, again, just stick with it until you are ready to tackle bigger changes.

Although there will be an initial stab of emotional pain, accepting the change instead of fighting it will enable you to prevent holding on to that pain.

True Acceptance

An alternative to resistance is acceptance, particularly self-acceptance. Difficult situations cause difficult emotions. For instance, if you try to blame others instead of accepting the situation, you are only resisting the problem. Acceptance allows you to feel the emotions surrounding a situation and recognize that these emotions are justified for the situation at hand, which frees you to move forward.

It's crucial to understand that acceptance isn't the same as giving up. If you want to free yourself from financial stress, acceptance means understanding that your current situation is temporary and you won't be poor forever. Again, this frees up energy that can be put toward planning financial goals. Accepting situations without judgment is known as radical acceptance, a core skill practiced in dialectical behavior therapy.

Not all situations are suitable for acceptance or radical acceptance. You shouldn't rely on radical acceptance when it means staying in unhealthy situations, whether professional or personal. This especially applies to relationships involving physical or emotional abuse.

Mindfully Embracing the Unknown

Mindfulness is a great tool for practicing acceptance because it keeps your mind in the present, allowing you to distance yourself from difficult emotions that arise with change and treat yourself with kindness and compassion. Even just a few minutes of mindfulness can give you the time to reduce the intensity of your emotions so that you can make mindful choices.

If you feel that your body is responding to change as if it were a threat, it's time to calm the amygdala so that your rational mind can work through the realities of change.

Take a few deep breaths to activate the parasympathetic nervous system, and consider if this change is within your control. If it is out of your control, it's a good moment to practice radical acceptance. If it is within your control, treat the change as an opportunity to practice your decision-making skills and weigh up the different ways you can handle this change so that you thrive rather than feel trapped in the impossible.

Self-Care for Physical and Mental Strength in the Face of Change

In times of uncertainty, self-care will take you a long way. Uncertainty can put added strain on your mental and physical self. The idea of taking care of ourselves, our basic needs, and even our wants can feel selfish.

However, self-care is the absolute opposite of being selfish. You can't pour from an empty cup, and you can't take care of your loved ones and accomplish your responsibilities if you aren't looking after yourself. Trying to cope with the stress and anxiety that stem from uncertainty will be more challenging.

Self-care isn't about indulgence, shopping trips, and hours at the spa. It can be as simple as preparing a healthy meal, reading your book, detoxing from technology, or enjoying a long walk in a peaceful forest. Self-care is different for everyone, so listen to what your body tells you.

Anxiety that comes from uncertainty is no different from other causes of anxiety, which means there will be triggers to identify. Today, the media has taken the negativity bias to new levels, and the additional emphasis on the negatives and disaster can fuel your uncertainty. You may also discover that your pessimistic outlook due to negative thoughts can blow change and uncertainty out of proportion.

Though we have already looked at how to reframe negative thoughts and break negative thought loops to make optimal choices, a different strategy may be necessary.

STRATEGY # 28: BREAKING NEGATIVE THOUGHT LOOPS

Cognitive distortions such as black-and-white thinking, catastrophizing, and fortune-telling are all forms of automatic negative thoughts that need to be analyzed for evidence and then rephrased to reflect the truth and be of more use.

At this point, you may have had some success at reframing cognitive distortions, but because this is a skill that requires practice, you may have also noticed that the same thought can get replayed as if stuck like a broken record.

Negative thought loops can not only cause increased stress and anxiety but also impact the way you view yourself and how you make decisions. It's one thing to tell yourself you are not good enough a handful of times, and it's another thing to repeat this thought continuously.

It's easy to say, "Look for the positive," but if you have ever been stuck in this type of thought loop, you will know that it's as much use as a chocolate teapot. Before you can try any technique to stop the thoughts, you need to break the loop.

Physically Snap Yourself Out of the Thought Loop

This is where the rubber band technique can help. When negative thoughts develop into a loop, you can flick the elastic band hard enough to snap your brain out of the loop but not too hard that you cause any real physical pain. It should be enough for your subconscious to want to avoid the stimulus.

The elastic band isn't a way to bury or ignore the thought. It is a distraction that can give you a chance to move on to other methods and revisit the thought when you feel you aren't going to get caught up in the loop again. You can also try firmly patting your body or clapping your hands. These actions suddenly stimulate your nerves and can break your anxious thought patterns. Try using it simultaneously with visualizing a stop sign.

Before moving on to the methods that prevent you from falling back into the thought loop, there is some caution to bear in mind with the rubber band technique.

First of all, make sure the band isn't so tight that it stops proper circulation. Also, it's empirical that flicking the band doesn't become an act of self-harm or replace other forms of self-harm.

Process Your Thoughts

Take a piece of paper and write down everything that is racing through your mind. You can do this as a brain dump without any structure, or you can answer specific questions on the negative thought loop.

• What was the origin of the thought loop?

• What were you doing at the time?

• How did the thought loop escalate?

• How is this thought loop affecting your body?

• Specifically, list the emotions that are caused by this thought loop.

• For each step of the escalation, where is the evidence to support your thought loop?

• Taking a step back, what would a friend tell you about each of the negative thoughts in the loop?

• Once you have physically "snapped" yourself out of the thought loop, it's time to process the thought.

• Is there any way this thought loop is trying to keep you safe or benefit you?

135

• What would happen if you let go of the thoughts?

Self-Soothe

Self-soothing is a kind way to help prevent the mind from slipping back into the thought loop. As the name implies, what comforts you has to be individual as the same action may frustrate the next person.

You may have an object or a photo that brings about a sense of calm; it could also be a particular smell or texture. Some people find massaging their temples or even the soles of their feet to be soothing.

Actively Find the Positive

You can now begin to look for the positive, even if it's the smallest, simplest act, like a few moments of mindfulness. Right where you are, spend a little time looking around for something that makes you smile or brings you a little joy. Is there someone nearby who you know you can rely on, a photo of a fond memory, or a video that improves your mood?

Just as negative thoughts can spiral into larger ones, so can the positives. Start with one thing that gets the metaphorical ball rolling. Then, you can move on to the amazing and proven gratitude practice.

A study in 2008 used MRIs to measure brain activity. Those who practiced gratitude showed activation in various areas of the brain, including the hypothalamus and the reward pathways. Practicing gratitude encourages the production of dopamine. As we have seen, thanks to neuroplasticity, the more we practice gratitude, the easier it is to retrieve these positive thoughts.

Gratitude journaling is something that only requires a few minutes a day, so it can be integrated into your routine. Even if you aren't actually writing, take a few moments during the day to consider these journal prompts:

- What is your favorite moment of each day?

- Name 5 things you are thankful for in the last 24 hours.

- What mistake have you made that you are grateful for (because you were able to learn)?

- Who deserves a thank you note in your life? Send one to them.

- What made you smile today?

- How have you grown as a person in the last 12 months?

- What skill do you have that you are grateful for?

- What is one personality trait you are thankful to have?

- What was the last act of kindness you did for someone else?

- List 5 things about your home and neighborhood you are grateful for.

There are many opportunities to practice gratitude with a friend, partner, or the whole family. As we have hopefully ditched using mobile phones at mealtimes, there is now a silence that can be filled with things you are grateful for.

One way to encourage openness about problems and difficult feelings is to play the "best and worst moments of the day" game. This game helps balance the negative elements of the day with positive ones.

If there is an area you have in common, you could create a gratitude board and regularly post positive messages, things to be thankful for, or phrases that make each other smile.

A gratitude jar is a great family activity where everyone adds a note each day. When the jar is full, you can go back and remind yourself of all the wonderful things in life. The gratitude board and jar can also be something you do for yourself.

Remember that balance is essential for this strategy to have the most impact. Take the example of 5 things to be grateful for in your home and neighborhood. If you can only think of three, that's fine.

Don't push it so that you risk the last two becoming toxic positive statements. At the same time, if you can only think of three after a few minutes, don't give up just yet because even the mundane can be something to be grateful for.

Optimal choices will only have a lasting impact if you can develop these strategies into long-term habits. In the penultimate chapter, we will uncover three strategies to make sure you make the best choices today, tomorrow, and for years to come.

CHAPTER EIGHT: F: FIRM HABITS

Whether it's New Year's or any other time, most of us have committed to good intentions only to revert to old ways after a few days—if that! One study published in the *European Journal of Social Psychology* stated that it takes an average of 66 days before a new behavior becomes a firm habit (Lally et al., 2009).

Though this may seem like a long time, it is just over two months to master the gripping habit of overthinking, which has probably consumed your life for years. The following three strategies are about taking what has been developed so far and making sure it sticks for many years to come.

STRATEGY #29: ESTABLISHING FIRM HABITS FOR LASTING CHANGE

If you consider a typical day, how much would you say is based on habit, those small actions, and the decisions you make? Habits range from making your morning drink to the order you put your clothes on. As with most things in life, our habits can be good or bad. Anything that drains you of your time and energy, affecting your physical and mental health, is a bad habit.

Unfortunately, you can just stop a bad habit. It's more likely that you will replace it. This is much the case when a person stops smoking only to find themselves eating more. Rather than reaching for a cigarette, they reach for a snack. It's easy to beat yourself up for this, but remember, habits are automatic.

The irony of the human psyche is that while we resist change when it comes to our bad habits, we seem to aim for big changes straight away. Because the brain is set up to prevent such enormous changes, we set ourselves up for failure. So, regardless of the habit you're trying to break, there are two fundamental rules to always have in mind:

1. Start small because there is always time to improve
2. The bad habit you want to stop needs to be replaced with a good habit

These two rules apply to overthinking, making optimal choices, or taking steps to a healthier lifestyle. Let's look deeper at how to successfully change habits for lasting change.

Automatic habits stem from triggers. The glass of wine you may reach for at the end of the day could be a way to escape from your overthinking. When reaching for your phone to check social media, is it because you have fallen into the habit of procrastination?

Before attempting to resolve the bad habit, you now have strategies to identify and prevent triggers from escalating.

To combine the fundamental rules, you can use a method known as habit stacking, and understanding neuroplasticity will help understand the effectiveness of this strategy. Each thought and action we carry out creates a connection between neurons that strengthens as we repeat it. Habit stacking allows the brain to connect synapses in stages so that each one gains strength before another stage is added.

Let's say you wanted to add 5 minutes of deep breathing to your daily routine. You would link this with another daily routine that is already established.

The simplest example would be your first cup of coffee in the morning! Once you have finished the coffee, stack the deep breathing onto your routine. The synapses in your brain are already wired for coffee preparation, so it's a case of adding one more connection rather than creating an entirely new set of connections.

Habit stacking can be used for any action you want to include in your day, making things more automatic. It can be walking away from your desk after a certain task, preparing clothes for the next day, or adding one more yoga pose to your routine.

Remember that your habits will always come down to the 3 Rs: Reminder, Routine, Reward. There will always be a trigger for your habit, the reminder. Next comes the routine or the action you carry out, and finally, there is a reward. If you take your morning coffee, the trigger is the need for caffeine, the routine is making and drinking the coffee, and the reward is the energy boost. As long as the reward is positive, the action will be repeated.

The 3 Rs also apply to bad habits, so it's essential to determine your triggers. If your habit is smoking, it's likely that the trigger is stress. Aside from taking steps to reduce stress, you can also find a way to stop the reward, for example, smoking a brand of cigarettes you don't like.

Finally, goals and habits aren't the same, so try to keep a distinction between the two. You might set a goal to lose 5 pounds, and to achieve this, you should set healthy lifestyle habits, starting with small, easy changes.

Once you lose 5 pounds, the healthy habits shouldn't stop. Instead, a new goal should be set, and more habits should be introduced, stacking them with healthy habits to achieve even more! Habits lead to routine, and routines give you the chance to achieve your goals!

STRATEGY #30: DEVELOPING POSITIVE ROUTINES

Have you ever noticed how your morning can set up your entire day? No matter how long it takes you to get out of the door, a smooth and unhurried start leads to a calmer and often more productive day. On the other hand, panic and stress can quickly have a snowball effect.

While a morning routine can significantly reduce stress, an evening routine can improve sleep, making the morning routine easier to stick to. Maintaining your daily routine allows time for self-care, exercise, and other healthy habits.

Waking up each day and knowing a plan is in place provides reassurance and stability. What's more, not having a routine can make you feel like you are not in control of your life, plus you have far more to think about!

It's impossible to create one morning routine that would work for everyone, but Hal Elrod discusses the S.A.V.E.R.S. method in his book *The Miracle Morning*. These six steps make for a solid foundation that you can adapt to suit your needs and lifestyle.

- **S: Silence** - Begin each day with a few moments of silence. Use this time for meditation, deep breathing, reflection, or setting intentions for your day.

- **A: Affirmations** - Use positive affirmations to start your day with the right mindset.

- **V: Visualization** - Visualize what you will achieve and the steps you will need to take to get there.

- **E: Exercise** - Mornings are great for exercise because it improves blood flow and gives your brain an oxygen boost for the rest of the day.

- **R: Reading** - Not scrolling through social media or a news app, but something that you can learn and grow from, something that will help you achieve your bigger picture.

- **S: Scribble** - Use that first drink of the day as the time to scribble down your thoughts, whether it's journaling, your to-do list, or the things you are grateful for.

Setting Up Your Own Routine

Although everyone's routines will look different, there is a logical process to help you get started:

1. Know what you need to do each day. Over the space of two weeks, write down absolutely everything you need and want to do. This should include everything from your habits to your responsibilities, and don't forget to include acts of self-care.

2. Ask yourself questions to better understand your own situation:

• When are you most active/productive during the day?

• How much of your time is required for work (including your commute)?

• Are there tasks on the list that depend on a partner or should be shared with a partner?

• If you have children, are they old enough to take on more responsibilities?

• Which tasks are daily, weekly, or monthly?

3. Understand how much time each task takes and be realistic about this. Don't forget to include the time you have for breaks if you are working.

4. Break your day up into chunks (e.g., before work, morning, lunch, afternoon, evening, before bed).

5. Organize tasks according to the chunk they should fit into, checking the estimated time for each activity so that you know you have time to complete everything within the chunks.

6. Check that each chunk contains a balance of things you need to do and things you want to do. You can use the "Sandwich Technique" to fit the less pleasant tasks in

between two things you enjoy. Also, check that high-energy tasks are scheduled for chunks where you feel more active throughout the day.

If you are looking at your list and feel that there isn't a balance between the things you need to do and those you want to do, it's certainly not going to be a positive routine that inspires you. Positive affirmations and visualization only take a few minutes, so they can easily be stacked with an existing habit you have.

Let's finish this strategy with ideas that go easy on your time and brighten up your day.

• Wake up early and avoid the snooze button

• Switch the morning social media scroll to stretching

• Listen to motivational music

• Listen to inspiring podcasts

• Eat the frog—do your hardest task first

• Solve a puzzle like a crossword or sudoku

• Do something nice for someone

• Take a moment to stretch

• Calm your mind with a brain dump

• Have a cold shower

• Mindfully drink a glass of water

• Spend time in nature

It's important not to contradict ourselves at this point. Having a routine, especially one that injects positivity into your day, has both physical and mental benefits, but routines can't be so strict that they don't allow for change. Your child might be sick and have to stay home from school, a parent might need your help, or you end up having to stay late at work.

Resisting these changes will only cause you mental turmoil. To reinforce your resilience and maintain healthy habits and positive routines, practicing mental stillness can keep you calm!

STRATEGY #31: CONSISTENCY IN PRACTICES FOR MENTAL STILLNESS

Mindfulness is a type of meditation, which is often a good starting point because focusing on sensory input can help calm the mind.

When practicing the grounding technique, for example, your attention is focused on your senses rather than distracting thoughts. This is not to say you block any thoughts that arise, but your attention is directed elsewhere.

Meditation is a more formal practice that requires being still while paying attention to a particular thought, object, or activity. Unlike the typical misconception, meditation isn't about emptying the mind but more about gaining mental clarity while calming emotions.

Meditation can bring about many of the same health benefits as mindfulness. They can improve sleep quality, help with pain management, and boost heart health by lowering blood pressure.

There have been several studies that support meditation for anxiety. An 8-week study showed reduced anxiety symptoms among those with generalized anxiety disorder (Hoge et al., 2014). Another 8-week study supported the use of meditation for anxiety and depression in those with chronic pain, and pain levels were reduced (Rod, 2015).

This is due to meditation's effect on the brain, but more specifically, the amygdala, the part of the brain responsible for the fight-or-flight response. Consistent meditation practice can shrink the amygdala and reduce its reactivity.

Moreover, this can reduce the inflammatory chemicals released in the brain when stress occurs, improving emotions. When participants in a separate study were shown negative images, those who engaged in meditation experienced fewer negative thoughts (Kiken & Shook, 2015).

Understanding the science behind meditation is crucial for developing the right mindset before you begin. If you start a meditation telling yourself it won't work, it won't! If you aren't feeling open to meditation at any point, it's best to return to it later, even if it's just an hour after you have ticked a few things off your list.

The reason many people give up on meditation, discount its advantages, or just don't even start is because they think it's necessary to sit in silence for long periods.

For anyone who struggles to sit still for 5 minutes without the mind racing, the idea of an hour would be ridiculous. Longer meditation sessions don't equal a greater impact. In fact, the benefits may even begin to decrease.

The best way to introduce meditation as a habit in your positive routine is to start with a few minutes at a time. Don't forget to incorporate it into an existing habit. You could start with a goal of 20 minutes and split this into 4 or 5 mini sessions throughout the day.

Here is a guide to help you begin your meditation practice.

1. Choose a location that is quiet, calm, and free from distractions. Choose a time when you know you won't be interrupted.

2. Set a timer for a few minutes. This way, your mind won't start questioning how much longer you have to go.

3. Find a comfortable position. The typical lotus position (crossed legs with each foot on the opposite thigh) is uncomfortable for many and will only distract you. You can sit on the floor or a chair, kneel or lie down.

4. Take a deep breath, follow that breath as it fills your lungs, and slowly inhale, noticing any sensations that come about. Continue to focus on your breathing.

5. When a thought comes to mind, accept it, don't attach any emotion to it, and know that you aren't going to obsess over it. Tell yourself to take a deeper breath, hold it longer, and exhale slower.

6. Once the timer goes off, don't move straight away. Take a moment to reflect. Notice how you feel, both physically and emotionally. Finish with a kind or grateful thought.

If you find that your mind is too easily distracted just with breathing exercises, there are other things you can focus on.

Candle meditation gives you the chance to concentrate on the flicker of a flame. Another option is to repeat a positive affirmation, either aloud or silently.

A few minutes soon become five, then ten, and meditation becomes easier. Even then, there will be times when mental distractions occur. Don't berate yourself for this—you are only human. Instead, be kind to yourself and know that it's not enough to reverse the benefits of meditation. At the same time, be accountable to your practice. Commit to regular practice and to getting better.

Calming the mind and reducing stress and anxiety isn't limited to meditation. Listening to music can have a profound impact on your mood, but dancing may even be better!

One thousand people participated in a study on free-form dancing, not following any set moves but just going with your own flow. Of the participants who suffered from anxiety and depression, 96 percent said unchoreographed dancing had a therapeutic effect (Laird et al., 2021).

On the other scale, many rewards can be reaped when we just learn to slow down! While walking and hiking are both excellent physical activities, take a moment to add a moment of forest bathing. This Japanese practice requires you to find a spot, sit down, and just take in the moment, focusing on your senses and environment. This can be combined with deep breathing, journaling, or positive affirmations.

Gardening might not be something you associate with mental health benefits, but research has found that soil contains a bacteria that acts as a natural antidepressant.

Mycobacterium vaccae triggers the release of the "happy hormone" serotonin (Francis, n.d.). Growing your own food, even if it's just some herbs, can also do wonders for your confidence and diet.

Lastly, go back to your list of things you want to achieve in a day and consider how many of them could be done with a more mindful approach.

Rather than taking a shower, going through the motions while the brain spins out of control, pay attention to the texture and scents of soaps and shampoos, adjust the temperature of the water, and notice the sensations on the skin, or listen to your favorite uplifting song. Even dreaded tasks such as cleaning, laundry, and ironing can all be improved with a touch of mindfulness.

I like to view firm habits as a bridge between the present and the future. Every effort I make to establish habits that lead to a more productive and happier day will make a positive difference in the future. And this is where our final step of the SWITCH OFF method takes us: a future filled with achievements and well-being.

CHAPTER NINE: F: FUTURE FOCUS

Travel to Sequoia National Park, and your first stop will probably be the General Sherman tree, the most huge tree in the world with a height of 274.9 feet. It has taken approximately 2,200 years to grow and reach a circumference of 102.6 feet (National Park Service, n.d.).

What's the secret of this impressive tree? Its ability to adapt and grow! We have taken time to explore the roots of overthinking in the past and the wonders of enjoying the present to calm the mind. Now, it's time to prepare for a fulfilling future!

STRATEGY #32: GROWTH MINDSET & ADAPTABILITY

The expression "You can't teach an old dog new tricks" has caused thousands, if not millions, of people to believe that they are incapable of developing new skills and acquiring new knowledge. This is known as a fixed mindset, a term coined by psychologist Carol Dweck.

Those with a fixed mindset see intelligence as being static, meaning there is no room for improvement. They will avoid challenges, even if there is an opportunity for growth, and when faced with obstacles, they will give up quickly because they can't see that the effort will be worth it.

It's possible that a fixed mindset leads to feeling threatened by other people's success, and even when offered feedback, they will only take this as criticism rather than helpful feedback.

According to Dweck, this isn't the only mindset. On the other hand, there are those with a growth mindset. These people don't believe you have to make the most of what you are given! They know the efforts they make, and more so when faced with challenges because they know that they will reach their goals through determination and persistence. People with a growth mindset are able to sift through criticism and take actions that will enable them to improve.

However, what stands out the most about the growth mindset is that they know their intelligence can be developed, and this links directly back to neuroplasticity. Now that you know how repeating thoughts and actions changes the structure of the brain, you can appreciate how intelligence can be changed and how old dogs, regardless of their age, can learn new tricks.

Throughout the previous strategies, we have seen how thought patterns can be changed by rewiring our brains. Telling yourself you are stupid over and over again reinforces the negative synapses in the brain. Replacing that thought with an affirmation strengthens the positive synapse, and over time, the negative synapse is replaced with a positive.

Neuroplasticity isn't just about replacing negative thoughts. Connections between neurons can begin with any thought, feeling, or behavior. Anything you want to learn begins with two neurons firing together. The more the learning is revised, the stronger that connection becomes, whether it's mastering DIY skills or learning how to code.

Neuroplasticity proves that we are all capable of self-development and attaining a growth mindset. Now that you know a growth mindset is possible, it's time to take steps toward developing one.

Know your purpose

Developing a growth mindset isn't about waking up one morning and deciding to make more effort. While you should praise yourself for your efforts toward all your achievements, for a genuine growth mindset, begin by understanding what motivates you to make changes. In what areas of your life do you want to see improvements, and what is the purpose of this change?

Embrace the learning experience

Growth requires learning, and this isn't always easy for adults, not just because of the lack of time but also because past experiences may not always be positive. On the one hand, you will need to learn specific skills to achieve more. On the other hand, before this, you need to appreciate a love of learning first! Begin by searching free online courses for a topic that excites you instead of something you feel you need to do.

Change your perspective on failure

Just as we say when making decisions, not everything is going to go as planned. Making mistakes is part of being human, and it's time to welcome your imperfections. The next time you catch yourself saying, "I made a mistake," rephrase it as "I made an opportunity." Everyone who has ever achieved greatness started as a child, full of enthusiasm rather than skill!

Stop looking for approval

When you seek approval from others, your goal becomes about being right or accepted based on other people's expectations, which prevents your growth. As a straightforward example, imagine only cooking certain meals because your partner loves them. This limits your opportunities to experiment with new recipes and explore your preferences.

Be active about feedback

Don't just wait for someone to provide you with constructive criticism. Although it can be nerve-wracking to ask others for their opinion, you will be pleasantly surprised. Because of the negativity bias, you will have assumed the worst. It's more likely that people have a lot of positive things to say about you, and the constructive criticism they do provide can make a great difference in your life.

Use the power of "yet"

I remember the first time one of my children came home from school with a crafts project. We were both excited, and I had created this expectation of what our project would look like. The reality was shocking, and I felt useless. The first thing I thought was, "I'm no good at this," and this was true. But that doesn't mean I can't improve as long as I keep working on my craft skills. So, I added just one word: "yet." Now I say, "I'm no good at this yet!"

While on the subject of learning, there are two more concepts that should be added to your skill set. The first is adaptability, the skill of adapting your thoughts and behavior to the changing environment around you.

Picture this as the step before resilience. You invested money in the stock market, and the value fell. There is nothing you can do to change the stock market, but you can change how you react. You have a choice between getting angry or learning from experts about alternative investments. Resilience enables you to bounce back and reinvest!

Take the following steps toward adaptability:

• **Work on your problem-solving skills:** Identify the problem, brainstorm various solutions, and consider the potential outcomes of each solution before settling on the best.

• **Be a calculated risk taker:** Taking risks gives you the chance to step outside of your comfort zone and see just how capable you are. In turn, these risks allow you to become more comfortable with change.

• **Keep an open mind:** It's normal to form thoughts and biases that prevent us from seeing things from different perspectives. New perspectives help with decision-making and problem-solving because you have more information.

Rather than letting your brain come up with these biases, focus your energy on active listening.

• **Don't let your ego get in the way:** If you put forward an idea and it's not chosen, it's normal to feel disappointed. If you let your ego take over, you will hang onto this disappointment. You will gain more by supporting the person whose choice was accepted and learning from them.

A positive outlook will make adaptability easier, and this is the second skill that should be added to your growth mindset arsenal. Psychology is very much focused on repairing the bad. Martin Seligman, the founding father of positive psychology, argues that we can change our outlook on life through learned optimism.

For physical health, optimism can improve the quality of life of those with chronic health conditions, lower the risk of high blood pressure and heart attacks, and prevent negative coping strategies such as smoking and alcohol consumption. Additionally, optimism can lower stress levels, increase perseverance, lead to better decision-making, and boost happiness at work.

To learn optimism, you can work on overcoming three cognitive distortions linked to the 3Ps.

1. Personalization is the cognitive distortion where anything bad that happens is internalized and the person's fault. An optimist will see that they aren't to blame and that things will be better next time.

2. Pervasiveness is linked to catastrophizing. When a bad thing happens, or a mistake is made, they are doomed for failure, often combined with sentences beginning with "I will never..." or "I will always be..." (contrary to the beliefs of those with a growth mindset).

3. Permanence is linked to things being unchangeable. Optimists can accept that they had a bad day or moment but know it is only the current situation. They will understand why they are off their game but also see that it's not permanent.

Learned optimism doesn't include blocking out pessimistic thoughts. Optimism allows you to express your entire range of emotions with a belief that the future is positive. It's not the same as toxic positivity, which forces only the good. To view things from different perspectives, you need to see the complete picture.

At the end of the day, take a few moments for reflection. Ask yourself what annoyed you and what was difficult about the day, but then ask yourself what you were proud of and what made you happy.

Even if you have firm goals set, with your newfound growth mindset and learned optimism, it's definitely a good idea to reassess your goals. And this takes us to our final strategy!

Strategy #33: Future Visualization and Goal Setting

Self-visualization or future visualization is a concept that originated in the sports world when athletes envisioned their future selves and their wins as part of their preparation for the right mindset.

Interestingly, this is one area where positive psychology and negative psychology meet. In ancient Rome, Stoic philosophers used to imagine negative outcomes of a situation to be better prepared. Future visualization takes this and combines it with optimism and positive outcomes.

Above all, future visualization is about being realistic about the future based on your expectations and nobody else's.

There is no fixed rule about how far ahead you should look, but generally, between 5 and 10 years gives you ample time to achieve some of life's bigger dreams.

Answer the following questions to gain a clearer image of how you visualize your future:

- Which country and city do you live in?

- What is your house like?

- Do you have a partner/children?

- What are you doing for a living?

- What is your financial situation?

- Are you debt-free?

- Do you have a passive income?

- What do you look like?

- How do you feel?

- What is your physical health like?

- How are you managing stress?

- Do you still have your core friends?

- What is your social life like?

- What impact do you have on other people's lives?

- Are you active in a faith or in your community?

These questions can't be answered vaguely. When you picture your future home, you need to go into as much detail as possible.

Does it have the island in the kitchen you always wanted? What type of floors do you have? Is it clean and simple, or busy and hectic? What's growing in your garden? Are you overlooking a beach or tucked away in the mountains?

The vision you have for yourself has to be motivating, so picturing any old roof over your head isn't going to drive you.

Now that you have your future visualized, it's important not just to abandon the idea. Spend 5 or 10 minutes a week reviewing the answers and creating the same vision to keep the excitement alive. Every 6 months, answer the questions again to see how much closer you are to the vision.

Even then, you can't solely rely on your imagination to achieve your visualizations. This technique allows you to use mental images to create and experience the emotions associated with your ideal life. Next, you need a plan to get there!

For direction, focus, clarity, greater motivation, and control over your future, you need goals. Goals are the final puzzle piece that takes the growth mindset, adaptability, and optimism to make the future visualization become a reality!

Essentially, you need to consider your short-term and long-term goals. One way to do this is to look at your future visualization and take ideas from that (for example, the kitchen with an island, to clear the credit card debt, or pay

X amount off the mortgage). The short-term goals can be those you want to set for the next 6 months in order to see progress toward your ideal future life.

It's likely that you have come across SMART goals, but there is a way to set your goals the SMARTER way!

• **S**pecific: Specific goals take a vague idea, narrow the focus, and create clear expectations of what will be achieved.

• **M**easurable: As the expression goes, if you can't measure it, you can't manage it. When metrics are used, it's easier to monitor progress.

• **A**chievable: Your goals have to be realistic. If you are 5 feet tall, it's unrealistic to have a goal to become an NBA GOAT—Greatest of All Time. Remember the Goldilocks effect, where there should be a midpoint between two extremes, hard enough to make it a challenge but not too hard to make it impossible.

• **R**elevant: Make sure your goals align with your values, purpose, and visualized future. While it's great to help others toward their goals, your own goals need to be focused on you!

• **T**ime-bound: There has to be a deadline for goals so that you can hold yourself accountable.

• **E**valuated: This goes beyond the planning stage and examines how you interact with your goals on an ongoing basis. What habits have you managed to implement that are helping you progress toward your goals? This is an important step because it teaches you to see that the focus of a goal should be on the process, not the end result, and that each day, you are growing.

• **R**evised: Here, we go back to celebrating our imperfections as well as embracing adaptability and resilience. It's not always going your way, and things may come up that throw you a curveball. If you can honestly say that you did everything possible to reach a goal, but external factors prevent it from happening, it's okay to revise your goals during evaluations.

I can't emphasize enough the importance of setting SMARTER goals that are in line with your values, as this will provide you with the motivation to stay on the right path. Happiness is a core value, so let's stick with this one.

There is a huge societal expectation as to what happiness means. To be happy, you need to graduate, get a goal in your ideal career, get married, buy a house, and have 2.4 children. There is absolutely nothing wrong with setting this as your goal if that is what you have envisioned as your future. But don't start working toward this goal if your idea of happiness is backpacking around the world alone!

The biggest question is what to do when responsibilities and life sweep us away, and our goals get put on the back burner. There are two things that can act as a physical, even visual reminder of our goals. The first is a vision board, and the second is a goal tracker.

The vision board allows you to tap into your creativity by making a visual representation of your future self. Imagine driving past the house of your dreams, take a photo, and add it to your board. If there is an image of your dream holiday, print it off.

Quotes that motivate you, things that make you smile, and anything that feels like a part of your positive future can be added to a vision board, and this board can then be hung in a place where you spend a lot of time, at least so it's seen every day.

For your goal tracker, I keep two. One is a digital copy that tracks long-term goals. I update this each month based on a hard copy of my short-term goals and a monthly calendar that is also kept in a highly visual place, such as next to the vision board or on the fridge!

The combination of the vision board and the goal trackers ensures your goals, dreams, and aspirations remain a priority and are not left sitting in the bottom of a drawer!

After 32 other strategies, your overthinking now seems like a distant past. However, because we are only human, it's possible that every now and then, there will be moments when the brain attempts to take over again and lead you down the negativity trap. If this does happen, take advantage of your goal trackers, especially your vision board.

Use these inspiring images as the focus of a short meditation session, adapt the grounding technique, and imagine what your senses tell your future self. Remind yourself that your future holds incredible potential and joy, regardless of your past!

CONCLUSION

Anyone who doesn't overthink will never truly understand just how debilitating it is. For them, it's like biting your nails or not making the bed in the morning. How hard can it be?

You may have come across people who imply you are simply bored, and this is why your brain doesn't stop. As if having more to do will stop the constant noise in your mind.

They don't understand how overthinking has gripped every aspect of your life, from how you view yourself to your ability to make decisions and even function on a daily basis. They can't imagine the emotional exhaustion you feel and how this stress and anxiety consumes you. Even those who think they understand what you are going through will rarely have the practical solutions to stop overthinking.

Over the last 9 chapters, you have undergone a transformation like no other, and though the journey is just beginning, even after the first step, understanding more about your thought patterns has provided you with the clarity you needed.

Someone as simple as knowing how the human brain is wired for negativity as a way to protect us can offer much-needed relief. Another thing that provided me with so much reassurance was neuroplasticity and the science of how we can literally change our brains with such simple techniques as positive affirmations.

Overthinking is naturally associated with the brain, but thanks to the vagus nerve, you now appreciate the holistic approach to overcoming overthinking. The mind and body are not two separate entities that require different healing strategies but, instead, are intricately linked vessels, and the approach to overthinking can't be left to psychology alone.

Both your mind and body need physical activity, whether that's an hour in the gym or a yoga session. They require a healthy and balanced diet, preferably with foods that support cognitive function as well as gut health. The benefits of a nutritious diet can be enhanced by slowing down and savoring each bite you take instead of rushing each meal as if it were another task on the to-do list.

Speaking of the beauty of slowing down, there is no need to exacerbate the problem of a constantly racing mind. Time is a precious resource, and in the past, you may have felt that doing everything at top speed would eventually lead to more free time.

But how did that benefit you when the only thing you could do with your free time was overthink? You have discovered the science behind mindfulness and have the strategies. Take the steps to make mindfulness a daily habit!

The amazing thing about the 33 strategies in the SWITCH OFF method is that none occupy massive amounts of time, especially when you use habit stacking. If you are already in the habit of making your morning coffee, you only need to add one minute to fully appreciate the aroma, flavor, and bodily sensations that coffee can offer to experience the benefits of mindfulness.

It's the small acts of taking care of the mind and body that make those more challenging strategies all the more achievable. Giving yourself mental and physical energy is crucial in order to master cognitive reframing, genuine positive self-talk, breaking the negative thought loop, and developing emotional resilience.

Above all, practicing self-care is fundamental for setting those limits with others that will prevent people from draining you of all the efforts you make toward your personal growth and development. Neither self-care nor boundaries are selfish!

It's these techniques that pave the way for an optimal future. One where you have quietened the mental chatter so much that decisions are no longer an obstacle that fuels overthinking, when the inevitable stressful moments don't set you back, and when mistakes don't cause you to revert back to unhealthy habits.

At this point, the SWITCH OFF method converts into the SWITCH ON method, as if your future now has a new and much brighter light bulb illuminating it. Because overthinking is no longer holding you back, the dreams become possibilities, and those powerful habits that have got you this far are what will take you to the next stages of your life!

I'm not going to lie. Stress and overthinking aren't going to magically disappear. The goal of the SWITCH OFF method is to ensure you have the tools to handle anything that comes your way and with confidence. They teach you that these obstacles are minor bumps in the road of a much longer journey that doesn't have to be defined by negativity.

With these 33 strategies, you have everything you need to take back control of your life. Each of the strategies I have implemented in my own life, some having a far greater impact than others, but that's the beauty of individualism! It's because of these strategies that I found the strength to help others. And now, I ask you a similar favor.

Remember how you felt as you turned the pages of the introduction. There are so many other people who are forcing a smile on their faces as they feel helpless under the weight of overthinking. By sharing your opinions on Amazon, those people can see that there is an effective solution for them to break free from their pasts and embrace a fantastic future. I promise it will only take a few minutes, and this act of kindness will add another dash of positivity to your life!

Not that you need it, but good luck with all your future aspirations. I look forward to hearing your success stories!

CONTINUE YOUR JOURNEY WITH 'THE ART OF SELF-IMPROVEMENT' SERIES BY CHASE HILL

HOW TO STOP NEGATIVE THINKING

This guide breaks down **seven easy steps to tackle everything from fleeting intrusive thoughts to deep-seated ruminations.** With practical strategies, exercises, and tools, it helps you pinpoint the roots of your negative thoughts and offers proven techniques to calm your mind.

Learn how to **shed toxic behaviors and embrace self-love** and acceptance through positive affirmations and self-talk. If you're ready for a happier, more positive outlook, this guide is your starting point.

HOW TO STOP OVERTHINKING

Struggling with endless mental chatter and worst-case scenarios? You're not alone—73% of adults battle overthinking. This book offers a clear roadmap to freedom, packed with **over 60 techniques to stop overthinking**, calm your mind, and escape toxic thought patterns.

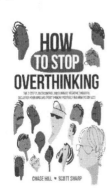

Learn quick, easy steps to calm an overactive brain, understand the dangers of rumination, and recognize the nine signs that you're trapped in a cycle of overthinking and how to break free before it's too late.

Discover how to relax your brain and handle toxic people. Ready to reclaim your peace and enjoy life? Dive into this essential guide and take control of your thoughts.

HEALTHY BOUNDARIES

Discover the power of self-love, and learn how to **set healthy boundaries – without feeling guilty**. You don't have to compromise your individuality just to be "considerate" of others. You can set healthy boundaries, and make your friends, family and parents **respect that boundary.**

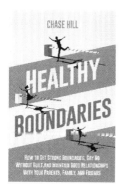

Setting up boundaries isn't about being rude: it's about acknowledging that **your well-being comes first.** You can start doing what YOU want to do.

––––––

READY FOR MORE INSIGHTS AND INSPIRATION? SCAN THE QR CODE TO FIND MORE BOOKS BY CHASE HILL AND CONTINUE YOUR JOURNEY.

BIBLIOGRAPHY

Akkasheh, G., Kashani-Poor, Z., Tajabadi-Ebrahimi, M., Jafari, P., Akbari, H., Taghizadeh, M., Memarzadeh, M. R., Asemi, Z., & Esmaillzadeh, A. (2016). Clinical and metabolic response to probiotic administration in patients with major depressive disorder: A randomized, double-blind, placebo-controlled trial. *Nutrition*, *32*(3), 315–320. https://doi.org/10.1016/j.nut.2015.09.003

Asp, K. (2022, July 11). *9 Health benefits of swimming*. EverydayHealth.com. https://www.everydayhealth.com/fitness/health-benefits-of-swimming/

Bradberry, T. (2014, January 9). Emotional Intelligence -EQ. *Forbes*. https://www.forbes.com/sites/travisbradberry/2014/01/09/emotional-intelligence/?sh=41d0be061ac0

Cherry, K. (2022, November 7). *What is the fight-or-flight response?* Verywell Mind. https://www.verywellmind.com/what-is-the-fight-or-flight-response-2795194#:~:text=3%20Your%20body%20can%20stay,it%20to%20pre%2Darousal%20levels

Das Graças Fedoce, A., Ferreira, F., Bota, R. G., Bonet-Costa, V., Sun, P. Y., & Davies, K. J. A. (2018, June 4). *The role of oxidative stress in anxiety disorder: Cause or consequence?* National Library of Medicine. https://www.ncbi.nlm.nih.gov/pmc/articles/PMC6218334/

Dean, J. (2023, January 3). *What happiness feels like physically in the body*. PsyBlog. https://www.spring.org.uk/2023/01/what-happiness-feels-like.php

Dighriri, I. M., Alsubaie, A. M., Hakami, F. M., Hamithi, D. M., Alshekh, M. M., Khobrani, F. A., Dalak, F. E., Hakami, A. A., Alsueaadi, E. H., Alsaawi, L. S., Alshammari, S. F., Alquhtani, A. S., Alawi, I. A., Aljuid, A. A., & Tawhari, M. Q. (2022, October 14). *Effects of omega-3 polyunsaturated fatty acids on brain functions: A systematic review*. National Library of Medicine. https://www.ncbi.nlm.nih.gov/pmc/articles/PMC9641984/#:~:text=Participants%20who%20received%20omega%2D3,blood%20flow%20in%20the%20brain

El-Khoury, J., Haidar, R., Kanj, R., Ali, L. B., & Majari, G. (2020). Characteristics of social media 'detoxification' in university students. *Libyan Journal of Medicine*, *16*(1). https://doi.org/10.1080/19932820.2020.1846861

Elrod, H. (2024). *The Miracle Morning (Updated and Expanded Edition): The Not-So-Obvious Secret Guaranteed to Transform Your Life (Before 8 AM)*. Simon and Schuster.

Francis, R. (n.d.). *Why gardening makes you happy and cures depression*. Permaculture College Australia. https://permaculture.com.au/why-gardening-makes-you-happy-and-cures-depression/#:~:text=Getting%20your%20hands%20dirty%20in,and%20strengthens%20the%20immune%20system

Grant, B. L. (2023, February 27). *Antidepressant microbes in soil: How dirt makes you happy*. Gardeningknowhow. https://www.gardeningknowhow.com/garden-how-to/soil-fertilizers/antidepressant-microbes-soil.htm#:~:text=Did%20you%20know%20that%20there%27s,makes%20you%20relaxed%20and%20happier

Harvard. (2020, September). *Mindful eating*. The Nutrition Source. https://www.hsph.harvard.edu/nutritionsource/mindful-eating/

Harris, R. (2008). *The Happiness Trap: How to Stop Struggling and Start Living*. Trumpeter.

Hewitt, J. (2017, July 12). *You are naturally biased to be negative. Here's how to change*. World Economic Forum. https://www.weforum.org/agenda/2017/07/you-are-naturally-biased-to-be-negative/

Hoge, E. A., Bui, E., Marques, L., Metcalf, C. A., Morris, L. K., Robinaugh, D. J., Worthington, J. J., Pollack, M. H., & Simon, N. M. (2014, February 1). *Randomized controlled trial of mindfulness meditation for generalized anxiety disorder: Effects on anxiety and stress reactivity*. National Library of Medicine. https://www.ncbi.nlm.nih.gov/pmc/articles/PMC3772979/

Hu, J., Zhang, J., Hu, L., Yu, H., & Xu, J. (2021). Art therapy: A complementary treatment for mental disorders. *Frontiers in Psychology, 12*. https://doi.org/10.3389/fpsyg.2021.686005

Hunt, M. G., Marx, R., Lipson, C., & Young, J. (2018). No more FOMO: Limiting social media decreases loneliness and depression. *Journal of Social and Clinical Psychology, 37*(10), 751–768. https://doi.org/10.1521/jscp.2018.37.10.751

Kiken, L. G., & Shook, N. J. (2015, December 1). *Does mindfulness attenuate thoughts emphasizing negativity, but not positivity?* National Library of Medicine. https://www.ncbi.nlm.nih.gov/pmc/articles/PMC4178287/

Lachance, L., & Ramsey, D. (2015, March). *Food, mood, and brain health: Implications for modern clinician*. National Library of Medicine. https://www.ncbi.nlm.nih.gov/pmc/articles/PMC6170050/#:~:text=Several%20nutritional%20deficiencies%2C%20such%20as,%2C%20cognitive%20decline%2C%20and%20irritability

Laird, K. T., Vergeer, I., Hennelly, S. E., & Siddarth, P. (2021). Conscious dance: Perceived benefits and psychological well-being of participants. *Complementary Therapies in Clinical Practice, 44,* 101440. https://doi.org/10.1016/j.ctcp.2021.101440

Lally, P., Van Jaarsveld, C. H. M., Potts, H. W. W., & Wardle, J. (2009). How are habits formed: Modelling habit formation in the real world. *European Journal of Social Psychology, 40*(6), 998–1009. https://doi.org/10.1002/ejsp.674

Larsen, J. T., Tiffany, A., Smith, N. K., & Cacioppo, J. T. (1998). Negative information weighs more heavily on the brain: The negativity bias in evaluative categorizations. *Journal of Personality and Social Psychology, 75*(4), 887–900. https://doi.org/10.1037/0022-3514.75.4.887

Levitin, D. J. (2014). *The Organized Mind: Thinking Straight in the Age of Information Overload.* Dutton.

Losinski, T. (2019, July 9). How walking fast can extend your life by 15 years or more. *Everything Zoomer.* https://www.everythingzoomer.com/health/2019/07/09/how-walking-fast-can-extend-your-life-by-15-years-or-more/

Magner, A. (2022, January 13). *How movement can help introverts 'Cure' overthinking.* IntrovertDear.com. https://introvertdear.com/news/how-movement-can-help-introverts-cure-overthinking/

Mark Twain Quote. (n.d.). A-Z Quotes. https://www.azquotes.com/quote/423413

Mbuthia, M. (2022, April 15). *70+ deep meaningful overthinking quotes to take your mind off things.* Legit.ng - Nigeria News. https://www.legit.ng/ask-legit/quotes-messages/1463501-70-deep-meaningful-overthinking-quotes-mind-things/

Medindia. (2021, October 20). *Antioxidant food chart - spices and herbs.* https://www.medindia.net/patients/calculators/antioxidant-food-chart-spices-and-herbs.asp

National Park Service. (n.d.). *The largest trees in the world - Sequoia & Kings Canyon National Parks (U.S. National Park Service).* https://www.nps.gov/seki/learn/nature/largest-trees-in-world.htm

Nijstad, B. A., De Dreu, C. K. W., Rietzschel, E. F., & Baas, M. (2010). *The dual pathway to creativity model: Creative ideation as a function of flexibility and persistence.* European Review of Social Psychology. https://doi.org/10.1080/10463281003765323

Open Colleges. (2016, September 12). *6 ways digital media impacts the brain.* https://www.opencolleges.edu.au/blogs/articles/6-ways-digital-media-impacts-the-brain

Oppland, M. (2016, December 16). *8 traits of flow according to Mihaly*

Csikszentmihalyi. PositivePsychology.com. https://positivepsychology.com/mihaly-csikszentmihalyi-father-of-flow/

ParentCo. (2022, February 28). *Understanding the fascinating link between anxiety and creativity.* ParentCo. https://www.parent.com/blogs/conversations/2023-understanding-fascinating-link-anxiety-creativity-kids-sake

Rausch-Phung, E., & Rehman, A. (2023, December 19). *How long should it take to fall asleep?* Sleep Foundation. https://www.sleepfoundation.org/sleep-faqs/how-long-should-it-take-to-fall-asleep

Research Gate. (n.d.). *Figure 1. Flow experience model of Mihaly Csikszentmihalyi [12].* ResearchGate. https://www.researchgate.net/figure/Flow-experience-model-of-Mihaly-Csikszentmihalyi-12_fig1_346709628

Rod, K. (2015, September 27). *Observing the effects of mindfulness-based meditation on anxiety and depression in chronic pain patients.* PubMed. https://pubmed.ncbi.nlm.nih.gov/26417764/

Santilli, M. (2023, March 10). How to Stop Overthinking: Causes and Ways to cope. *Forbes Health.* https://www.forbes.com/health/mind/what-causes-overthinking-and-6-ways-to-stop/#:~:text=It%20might%20feel%20like%20you,people%20ages%2045%20to%2055

Schmidt, K., Cowen, P. J., Harmer, C. J., Tzortzis, G., Errington, S., & Burnet, P. W. J. (2014, December 3). *Prebiotic intake reduces the waking cortisol response and alters emotional bias in healthy volunteers.* National Library of Medicine. https://www.ncbi.nlm.nih.gov/pmc/articles/PMC4410136/

Simon, K., McDevitt, E. A., Ragano, R., & Mednick, S. C. (2022). Progressive muscle relaxation increases slow wave sleep during a daytime nap. *Journal of Sleep Research, 31*(5). https://doi.org/10.1111/jsr.13574

Strickland, J. C., & Smith, M. A. (2014, July 10). *The anxiolytic effects of resistance training.* National Library of Medicine. https://www.ncbi.nlm.nih.gov/pmc/articles/PMC4090891/

The University of Vermont. (2013, December 19). *Inc. magazine cites UVM research on Mood-Boosting benefits of early exercise.* https://www.uvm.edu/news/story/inc-magazine-cites-uvm-research-mood-boosting-benefits-early-exercise

Viktor E. Frankl quotes. (n.d.). Brainy Quote. https://www.brainyquote.com/authors/viktor-e-frankl-quotes?__cf_chl_tk=tiq95tU0PFKGLgk-Li5.bq7jM6vv0j1gg2VsdMpt1Jmw-1700926500-0-gaNycGzNE3s

Wang, H., Jin, M., Xie, M., Yang, Y., Xue, F., Li, W., Zhang, M., Li, Z., Li,

X., Jia, N., Liu, Y., Cui, X., Hu, G., Dong, L., Wang, G., & Qi, Y. (2023). Protective role of antioxidant supplementation for depression and anxiety: A meta-analysis of randomized clinical trials. *Journal of Affective Disorders*, *323*, 264–279. https://doi.org/10.1016/j.jad.2022.11.072